Determinism in Śramaṇic Traditions

Theme of Cover: The game of Snakes & Ladders is symbolic of a man's journey in life and is devoted to 84 numbered squares illustrated with the notions of *karma* and *mokṣa*. The ladders denote virtues such as faith, generosity, humility and asceticism, while the snakes represent vices such as anger, theft, lust and greed. The last square represents the state of liberation. The ladders convey that virtues lead one to liberation and vices to a cycle of rebirths. The number of ladders is less than the number of snakes, which means the path of virtue is much more difficult to tread, than a path of vice.

Determinism in Śramaṇic Traditions

Editors

Shrinetra Pandey

Sanjali Jain

International School for Jain Studies
Pune

DK PRINTWORLD
Publishers of Indian Traditions

Cataloging in Publication Data — DK

[Courtesy: D.K. Agencies (P) Ltd. <docinfo@dkagencies.com>]

International Seminar on "Determinism in Śramaṇic Traditions (Particularly Jainism and Buddhism): Their Moral and Ethical Effects (2018 : Aligarh, India)

Determinism in śramaṇic traditions / editors, Shrinetra Pandey, Sanjali Jain. - Second revised edition.

pages cm

One paper in HIndi.

Papers presented at an International Seminar on "Determinism in Śramaṇic Traditions (Particularly Jainism and Buddhism): Their Moral and Ethical Effects, organized by International School for Jain Studies, New Delhi in collaboration with Mangalayatan University, Aligarh on January 11-12, 2018 at the auditorium of the university.

Includes bibliographical references and index.

ISBN 9788124611562

1. Free will and determinism - Religious aspects - Jainism - Congresses. 2. Free will and determinism - Religious aspects - Buddhism - Congresses. 3. Determinism (Philosophy) - Congresses. 4. Fate and fatalism - Religious aspects Jainism - Congresses. I. Pandey, Shrinetra, 1981- editor. II. Jain, Sanjali, 1992- editor. III. International School for Jain Studies (New Delhi, India), organizer, publisher. IV. Mangalayatan University, organizer, host institution. V. Title.

LCC BL1356.I58 2018 | DDC 294.42 23

ISBN: 978-81-246-1156-2

First appeared as e-book in 2020

Second revised edition published in 2022

Published by:

International School for Jain Studies

(A Division of Amar Prerna Trust)

C/o Firodia Hostel

844, BMCC Road, Shivaji Nagar

Pune - 411004 (Maharashtra)

e-mail: isjs.india@gmail.com

website: www.isjs.in

and

D.K. Printworld (P) Ltd.

Regd. Office: "Vedaśrī", F-395, Sudarshan Park

ESI Hospital Metro Station, New Delhi - 110015

Phones: (011) 2545 3975, 2546 6019

e-mail: indology@dkprintworld.com

Website: www.dkprintworld.com

Printed by: D.K. Printworld (P) Ltd., New Delhi

Preface to Second Edition

The first edition of this book *Determinism in Śramaṇic Traditions* was published in 2020 in e-book format and was available on our website (www.isjs.in) for the readers. Many of the readers do not feel comfort with electronic version of the books and always prefer a physical copy. Some of such scholars requested us for the physical copy to read and to place it in their libraries. Therefore, we decided to publish the second edition in hard copy format.

This second edition is not only a transformation from electronic version to physical version, we have made some significant changes also. In the first edition, we had given references as endnotes while in current edition, we have adopted the in-text style to refer the citations and notes as footnotes. Beside this, we have given proper references in every article at the end. We have also added a consolidated bibliography before the list of contributors. Word index is another property of this edition.

No book is ever free from error or incapable of being improved. I would be delighted to receive comments, positive or negative, and corrections from you, the reader. You can send your suggestions to me at: dr.snpandey1981@gmail.com.

I am thankful to our Chairman Dr Abhay Firodia and our President Dr Shugan C. Jain for their guidance and to allow me to work on the second edition of the book. Thanks are also due to my colleague at ISJS Mr Sushil Jana for his technical support.

I am also thankful Mr Susheel Mittal and the staff at D.K.

Printworld who worked hard to bring out this edition. I hope that this book will serve as a resource for understanding the philosophy of determinism in Śramaṇic traditions.

7 April 2022

Shrinetra Pandey, PhD
Joint Director
International School for Jain Studies
(A Division of Amar Prerana Trust), Pune
Email: dr.snpandey1981@gmail.com

Preface to First Edition

The human life and cosmic world are full of diversities. Every person tries to know these diversities. In this process of understanding these diversities, so many questions arise in the mind. One of the important questions is as how our life is regulated. Are we regulated by destiny (*niyati* or *prārabdha*)? Or are we regulated by our own free will (*puruṣārtha*)?

Fatalism, determinism and pre-determinism (Niyativāda) are the terms generally used interchangeably. Fatalism is a philosophical doctrine stressing the subjugation of all events or actions to fate. Determinism, in philosophy, implies that all events, including moral choices, are completely determined by previously existing causes. Pre-determinism, a specific type of determinism, articulates that every single event or effect is caused by an uninterrupted chain of events that goes back to the origin of the universe.

Jain, Bauddha and Ājīvaka belong to the Śramaṇa tradition. Ājīvakas were firm believers of fatalism. But when we talk about *niyati* as per Jain perspectives, there is the doctrine of *karma*. According to the *karma* theory, an individual's present condition is determined not by any absolute principle but by his own actions performed either in his past lives or in the present life. By freely choosing the right course and following it faithfully, he could modify his destiny and ultimately attain liberation. In accordance with their well-known doctrine of Syādvāda or Anekāntavāda, do not totally reject the doctrine of Niyativāda. In the *Sanmatitarka Prakaraṇa*, Ācārya Siddhasena talks of five co-factors (*pañca-*

samavāya): *kāla*, *svabhāva*, *niyati*, *pūrvakṛta* and *puruṣa*. Any one of these co-factors, when taken singly, is false but true when they are considered jointly.

The Buddhist text *Dīgha Nikāya* talks of two types of determinism:

1. theistic determinism (*issaranimmānahetu*), and
2. kammic determinism (*pubbekatahetu*).

The *Aṅguttara Nikāya* says, "Don't blame me, it is the will of God" or inactivity, "What can I do? It's my past *kamma*." On the other hand, the *Buddhacarita* points out:

> If God is the cause of everything that happens, and then what is the use of human striving?

However, the Buddha does not teach that we have complete freedom or that we are determined, but that our will is conditioned or limited to a greater or lesser extent.

It is against these Śramaṇic expositions on determinism/ Niyativāda, International School for Jain Studies, New Delhi organized a two-day international seminar on "Determinism in Śramaṇic Traditions (Particularly Jainism and Buddhism): Their Moral and Ethical Effects" in collaboration with Mangalayatan University, Aligarh on 11-12 January 2018. The seminar was organized at the newly-built modern auditorium of Mangalayatan University.

The overall response from the academic community was very encouraging with thirty-three papers received from scholars and the distinguished address by Pt. Dr Hukam Chand Bharil, a strong proponent of fatalism in Śramaṇa tradition and from the top academic management of the Mangalayatan University. The response was so overwhelming that twenty-eight scholars could present their papers for discussions. We also had five papers which could not be presented in seminar but were distributed and informally discussed.

The proceedings of this seminar form the basis of this book in which ten papers, duly reviewed by academicians, are selected for publishing. Details of speakers and their papers along with the papers which could not be presented are given at the end. Similarly a consolidated bibliography is also given for further reference.

We are also thankful to all the contributors of articles contained in this volume. We also thank the scholars who presented very good papers in this seminar but the same could not be included here due to management constraints.

Organizing this seminar was a mammoth task. During the course of organizing the seminar we were indebted to a number of people. We sincerely express our gratitude to all of them. I express my heartfelt thanks to Dr Shugan C. Jain, Chairman, International School for Jain Studies for his guidance and support to make this seminar academically rewarding and promote fraternity amongst scholars participating in the seminar. I also thank Brig. (Dr) P.S. Siwach, Vice-Chancellor, Mangalayatan University, Aligarh for his guidance in different phases of organizing the seminar. My special thanks to Professor Jayanti Lal Jain (Dean, Humanities & Director Centre for Philosophical Studies, Mangalayatan University, Aligarh) and his team for their outstanding contribution in organizing facilities at Mangalayatan University.

Thanks are also duc to Ms. Sanjali Jain who accepted our request to edit this seminar transactions with me. Finally, I thank my colleagues at ISJS, Mr Sushil Jana and Ms Jyoti Pandey who did all word processing and electronic compiling of the seminar proceedings.

10 August 2020

Shrinetra Pandey, PhD
Joint Director
International School for Jain Studies
New Delhi

Contents

Preface to Second Edition v

Preface to First Edition vii

1. Determinism in Science and Jainism 1
   — *Surendra S. Pokharna*

2. Determinism and the Karma Theory of Jainism 17
   — *Prakash C. Kanthaliya*

3. Niyativāda in Jain Tradition 31
   — *Shugan C. Jain*

4. Free Will in Jainism 45
   — *Christopher K. Chapple*

5. Concept of Free Will in Theravāda Buddhism 75
   — *Bimalendra Kumar*

6. "Śramaṇa Ethics" Determinism in the Contemporary Context 83
   — *Meenal Katarnikar*

7. Free Will in the Realm of Morality: A Jain Perspective 97
   — *Kamini Gogri*

8. Niyativāda as Depicted in Jainism 109
   — *Navin K. Srivastav*

9. Determinism, Free Will and Morality: A Jain Perspective — 119
— Jinesh R. Sheth

10. नियतिवाद और कथंचित् नियति — 133
— राहुलकुमार सिंह

Summary of Presentations in Seminar — 143
— Shrinetra Pandey

About Organizing Institutions — 149

Consolidated Bibliography — 151

Contributors — 159

Index — 163

1

Determinism in Science and Jainism

Surendra S. Pokharna

Science, technology and their use in economic development and commercialization have revolutionized the world in such a way that everything appears to have changed in the last two centuries. Developments in the fields such as space technology, atomic energy, electronics, biotechnology, modern agriculture, telecommunication and manufacturing have brought changes to value systems, lifestyles, comfort levels, and the rich and poor divide. These changes have also played a key role in making the world into a so-called global village. However, they have also resulted in issues like an increase in population, depletion of natural resources, damage to the environment, increase in greenhouse gases, increase in terrorism and threats of nuclear wars.

If one looks at the state of our planet, one will find that half of the animals in the world have disappeared since 1970. The world has lost almost 25,000 biological species because of uncontrolled human activities (Knapton 1914; *How many species we are losing?* 2018). Every year, 150 billion animals are killed for food, which has damaging repercussions on the environment (*Animal kill counter*).

Due to new research fields like science and technology, many complex factors have arisen that determine the ultimate status and future evolution of a society. Here, one has to also emphasis that many of these factors like science, technology, economics, society, animal kingdom and environment are strongly interconnected in a very complex way. Unless the nature of these interrelations and interconnections is fully understood, one cannot correctly determine the status of the society and its members. Thus, it appears that the topic of determinism is a very complex one that needs to be understood afresh in the light of science-related developments.

Scientific methods developed to study physical systems like classical physics are not adequate when biological systems, social systems and human systems are considered because all biological systems are essentially irreversible in nature, that is they grow and decay, but they are also open systems as opposed to the physical systems which are closed systems. Thus, the biological and social systems cannot be strictly measured and, hence, they are not describable in physical sciences. Also, any type of experimentation is not possible in the case of human systems as they have memory, free will, creativity and a tendency to interact strongly with other fellow beings and the environment (Van Gigch 1978: 36-52, 57, 69). Furthermore, there are micro-controls in the form of thought processes which cannot be easily adjusted in any planned scientific experiment. They also have a property of infinite amplification because of the thought processes, which makes it difficult to study human beings in a strictly scientific way (Pokharna 2008, 2013a, b). It is now felt that the standard concepts used in any scientific study have their basis in compartmentalization, reductionism, causality, mechanism, induction, empiricism and passivism (Goldsmith 1990), so they cannot be used to strictly study biological and social systems in general and human systems in particular. Hence, even the study of the interaction of human systems with physical systems needs closer examination; not much can be stated about determinism in practical situations.

One solution is to explore the General Systems Theory (GST) for better understanding of the whole problem (Van Gigch 1978: 47-49), because by its intrinsic nature, GST can give a better picture of the interconnectedness of various components of the human–earth–atmospheric system. It is finally a problem of order and knowledge at all levels; the evolution of order, the development of order and the evolution of knowledge should be discussed for a complete understanding of determinism.

Limitations of scientific methodology are also brought into light through Godel's incompleteness theorems (Pokharna 2013b, Bhandari and Pokharna 2017: 23-24) which have compelled scientists to consider the concept of consciousness in a more serious way and also revise the concept of knowledge in a fundamental way. Thus, the concept of knowledge of Indian philosophy needs to be closely examined in view of the problems mentioned above. As per Indian philosophy, and especially Jain philosophy, knowledge is structured in the consciousness and what we discuss as scientific knowledge could be just a small part of this grand knowledge (Ācārya Nanesh 2008: 202-09; Bhandari 2015: 37-41). Hence, broader concepts of knowledge need to be explored to understand the concept of determinism.

Quantum physics studies reality at the subatomic level, involving electrons and photous which brings in additional complications inform of uncertainity in principle. Therefore, it is not even possible to determine the exact position and momentum of these particles even at one moment. If we try to determine one of them accurately then the other gets highly uncertain. Hence unlike classical physics, it is not possible to determine the trajectory of even one particle perfectly. When more than one particle is studied then the problem becomes still more complex. This is due to the dual nature of these particles. They show the particle aspect at one time and the wave aspect at another time depending on the experimental set-up used to study them. Hence, the description of these systems brings in other problems which come in the way of perfect determinism. The multiple states of a system and the associated probabilities determine what state a system will be found in. Therefore, it can be seen as a strong example of intrinsic indeterminism at a very fundamental level.

It has been recently observed that thought and decision-making processes in our brain follow rules similar to that of quantum mechanics. Hence, there can be a lot of uncertainty in an individual's decision-making process. Roger Penrose states that human decision making is neither deterministic, nor random, nor computable; it is, therefore, very fluid.

However, the Jain *karma* theory, involving the soul-matter interactions, provides a guiding principle for an individual about one's fate and one's controlled activities (Kachhara 2014). The concept of determinism in statistics is mentioned where determinism is always partial in nature. Some smaller topics like the practical use of statistics in day-to-day life are discussed. Furthermore, a model is given in which an abstract observer is defined for which causality is neither obeyed nor violated along with another entity which strictly obeys the law of causality perfectly. The interaction between the two is then discussed (Pokharna 1985). Lastly, a recent study by Neppe and Close (2012: 116-17) mentioned the concept of determinism and free will using multiple dimensions of time.

Scientific Measurement in Classical Physics

When one examines the scientific methodology, any phenomenon is called scientific if it can be verified in a laboratory under a given set of controlled conditions and it can also be reproduced at any place and point of time; this is called the space-time invariance condition.

In classical physics, if one assumes the whole universe consists of a large number of particles where the interactions (forces) among them are known and, therefore, the initial positions are known, then theoretically it is possible to know all past and future scenarios of these particles including their past or future positions and velocities. Of course, there will be several practical problems in knowing all these parameters for all the particles in the Universe, even at one time simultaneously. However, this would be a theoretical example of perfect determinism (Pokharna 1985).

The Relation between Science, Technology, Economics

There is also a need to go into the details of scientific methodology and how it is explored and exploited through technology and economics in the name of development. If one denotes a scientific experiment as Truth *A*, its conversion into technology as Truth *B*, the exploitation through economics in the name of development as Truth *C* and its total impact on the environment as Truth *D*, then the total truth (Truth *T*) of the system for this chain (one leading to the other) can be mentioned in the following way:

Scientific Experiment > Technology >
Economic Development > Environment

Truth *A* + Truth *B* + Truth *C* + Truth *D* is called
Total Truth, i.e. Truth *T*

Thus, Truth *A* is a small truth (subset) as compared to Truth *T*, in this chain of truths. Hence, when a scientist is performing an experiment, the rest of these truths are treated as indeterminate. However, the reality is not this because these indeterminate truths for a scientist are part of another type of reality involving technologists, economists, industrialists and environmentalists. As one moves from left to right in the above equation, more and more information is added up. Therefore, the total truth will be much more than the one implied by Truth *A* of the scientific experiment. It is the cumulative effect of science, technology and economics (being treated as the concept of development) that needs to be studied to know the total deterministic effect of science on the society and the environment (Pokharna 2013b).

Closed Systems, Interactions, Conservation Laws

Conservation laws of physics are defined as the foundation of all scientific measurements. This explains the existence of conservation laws for notions such as energy, linear momentum and angular momentum. These are defined for isolated closed systems by approximating their nature. For example, the energy is defined as that variable for a closed isolated system which does not change over time (Pokharna 2008, 2013a, b). Yet, in principle, we can never have a totally closed isolated system. Similarly, linear momentum is defined as that property of a closed isolated system which remains invariant with respect to any spatial displacement. Lastly, angular momentum is defined as the parameter for an isolated closed system which remains unchanged due to rotation in space. Hence, the mere definitions of conservation laws are such that interaction (electromagnetic, gravitational) is neglected. However, the interaction among systems is then studied by considering the nature and magnitude of the interaction. Hence, there is an intrinsic element of indeterminism in the basic definition of our scientific understanding of a phenomenon. They may not be the accurate choice to describe reality in general, especially in the biological and social systems, where interactions are very predominant.

Open Systems, Entropy, General Systems Theory

For biological systems, which are always interacting with each other, classical physics' philosophy cannot be applied in a satisfactory way. All living beings are essentially irreversible in nature, in which they grow and decay, and they are also open systems, compared to the classic physics' theory in which they are closed systems (Van Gigch 1978: 40-41). These open systems constantly interact with the environment like human beings, who take information and oxygen from the atmosphere and release carbon dioxide and other waste products. A relative order is maintained in them through this process. Human systems also have memory, free will, creativity, and a tendency to interact strongly with other fellow beings and the environment. Furthermore, there are microcontrols, such as thought processes, which cannot be easily adjusted in planned scientific experiments. They are also goal-directed systems and so here the effect determines the cause and not vice versa, which is true for physical systems. Hence, biological systems, human systems and social systems cannot be subjected to the same process of measurement and hence they are not strictly describable in classic physics (Pokharna 2013b).

It is difficult to perform experiments on human systems and predicting events about them from a purely scientific perspective. Therefore, such systems are studied in a different way by using statistical procedures. In such procedures, only some rough trends or patterns can be found. Hence, these living systems are better studied using the General Systems Theory (Van Gigc 1978: 41-42). Here, entropy and information are very important, energy is secondary. This is a different type of determinism since a different approach is being used to study these systems. Here, spiritual evolution is more important and so determinism is accompanied by an increase in the system's order.

Quantum Physics

Quantum physics provides a new way of looking at reality; any sub-atomic particle like an electron or a photon can demonstrate either a wave aspect or a particle aspect. It all depends on the type of the experiment being designed to study these particles (interference or photoelectric effect). When one aspect (wave) is known, then the other (particle) appears to be indeterminate and vice versa (Kothari 1985). Also, as per classical physics, if the initial spatial coordinates and momentum of a particle are known then its location in future can be determined using Newton's laws of motion, either in the presence of a force or in its absence. However, in quantum physics, both location and momentum of a particle are uncertain and are governed by the Heisenberg uncertainty principle, through Planck's constant. If one is known accurately, then the other becomes highly uncertain and vice versa.

Actually, the state of a particle is determined by Schrodinger's equation using the probability function, known as the wave function, which describes only the probability of finding a particle at a given location (and not the actual value). Hence, there is an in-built uncertainty in the description of determining reality or the knowledge of reality, so that one does not know the actual reality. One only knows what the process of measurement and the methodology to communicate about reality, but they do not know the actual reality.

There is another way to describe a quantum system, which can exist in a superposition state, consisting of several eigenstates, such that when an experiment is conducted to understand the system then in the process of measurement, the superposition state reduces into one of the possible eigenstates, depending on the experimental set-up designed. The quantum formulation provides just probability of finding a system in one of the possible eigenstates. Now, some information is obtained about one of the eigenstates in an experiment as other information is lost.

Human Decision Making Is Neither Deterministic, Nor Random, Nor Computable

According to Roger Penrose, human decision making is neither deterministic nor random, but non-computational. It shows the inability to say anything about reality, where a kind of indeterminism is in-built into the intrinsic decision-making process itself (Paulson 2017). It may be therefore inferred that the concept of indeterminism is essentially in-built into the process of doing anything or any action. At the beginning of the twenty-first century, it was recognized that some experiments related to the human decision-making processes could not be explained by the conventional decision theory but could be explained by the models based on quantum mechanics and the mathematical formalism in it (Buchanan 2011). This new finding will have far-reaching consequences on the way humans look at the world and the methodology of describing anything, including modern science. The concept of determinism is, therefore, far-reaching.

Soul–Matter Interaction in Jainism

The *karma* theory of Jain philosophy deals with the soul–matter interaction. Jainism has defined the individual souls as the basic constituents of all living beings. A soul has the following properties: infinite knowledge, infinite intuition, infinite bliss and infinite power. Yet, from an infinite time in the past, it has been infected by matter. This matter has been held responsible for the disorder present in the worldly souls. This form of matter has been termed *karma*, which in Jainism does not mean work, but a very fine category of matter. The whole universe is full of that kind of matter which can become *karma*. Due to the presence of different types of *karma*s in different quantities, different characteristics are manifested by worldly souls. However, these *karma*s actually obstruct the true powers of a pure soul (Kachhara et al. 2017; Pokharna 2015).

At every moment, an empirical soul is attracting this matter towards it by its actions in the mind and body. This matter, which has now become *karma*, remains latent (in memory) in the empirical soul for a time. It is determined by the passions at the time of arrival of new matter. Passions in turn are determined by *karma*s which are already attached to the soul and some other conditions around the person. *Karma*s have the following four characteristics:

A. Nature,
B. number,
C. lifetime, and
D. intensity.

Essentially, this is one of the best models to determine the status of a person from several perspectives. The *karma* theory provides a very logical explanation of the concept of determinism for one's action and the fruit of one's actions, not only in this birth but for many births in the past, as well as those in the future.

Statistics

Statistics is an important branch of mathematics and is extensively used in studying many natural phenomena in physical, biological and social systems. Here, one takes a sample of data and then using the appropriate sampling, draws inferences about the probable total population. In simple cases, it is determined by some mean value and some standard deviation. As one increases the sampling fraction, one approaches more improved values, thereby improving the determinism. Here, determinism is never perfect and some uncertainty will always remain. However, for all practical purposes, it provides satisfactory results which are extensively used in widely different fields like agriculture, climatology, economics, environment, industries and politics. Thus, practically, simple approximate determinism is more than adequate for day-to-day applications. Similarly, disciplines like psychology and parapsychology also require statistics and, here too, determinism is only partial in nature but it is still useful.

The Object and the Observer

Generally, all studies in science and other fields are carried out on the assumption of separating oneself from the rest of the universe; that is the observer is treated as an entity which is a part of the universe and then the rest of the universe is studied. This separation will always lead to indeterminism because one's knowledge will always be incomplete. But in the field of spirituality and in almost all religions, this separation is to be avoided by merging oneself with the whole Universe. Thus, the observer merges with the object and there is no difference between the observer and the object. Then, higher stages of consciousness can be achieved through meditation; for example, it can open many new frontiers of knowledge, like telepathy and clairvoyance, which are not available during the normal stage of consciousness (Ācārya Nanesh 2008: 202-09). Hence, new types of knowledge may be discovered during the higher stages of consciousness. This provides new dimensions to the concept of determinism.

Variance of Determinism

Due to the above discussion, it appears that one can introduce a broad range of determinism starting from 0 per cent to 100 per cent. A situation of total chaos would have zero determinism, whereas, a perfect mathematical equation like Newton's law of motion will represent a situation of 100 per cent determinism. All other situations will fall in between these two extremes, like all statistical phenomena and quantum physics. Interestingly, one could ask whether the *karma* theory has 100 per cent determinism or below 100 per cent. Probably, when one attains *mokṣa*, 100 per cent detachment of *karmas* is required. Even 0.1 per cent or less *karma* will never allow a person to attain *mokṣa*. A perfect soul will have 100 per cent knowledge of the causal world, both of past and future, along with that of the present.

Perfect Determinism in a State of Omniscience

Due to these concepts of determinism, *karma* and the properties of the soul in Indian philosophy, Pokharna (1985) introduced an abstract entity for which causality is neither obeyed nor violated. The principle of causality points out that for every effect there is a definite cause behind it (or a large number of them) and every effect in turn becomes the cause of another effect. However, when one says that causality is violated then it can have the following three different meanings:

1. The cause and the effect have been temporally reversed so that we have the effect first and then the cause. This is the situation believed to exist in the case of tachyons, particles that move faster than light. They are assumed to move backward in time; thus, causality is violated by tachyons.

2. There may be some effects (or causes) whose causes (or effects) may not be known to us or no physically reasonable causes (or effects) can be searched for given effects (or causes). This situation is found in quantum mechanics, where some uncontrollable fluctuations exist in the state of predictability of a system in a given measurement process. These fluctuations are such that we cannot assign any known factors or causes responsible for them.
3. In the case of biological and social systems, where one always defines certain goals and then plans a set of activities such that the goal is achieved. In this case, the effect is fixed and defined in the form of a goal, and then causes are organized in such a way that the given goal is achieved.

Here, the relation between the cause and the effect does exist but the temporal relation is reversed in the sense that now cause does not determine the effect (natural time flow) but the effect determines the cause (time is somewhat flowing in the opposite direction to the conventional idea of time).

An attempt is made to study the problem of soul in an abstract way. The analysis has become an abstract formalism because of the underlying interest of the possibility of perfect determinism within quantum mechanics. Two abstract entities are introduced to deal with this problem. The first is an abstract causal world described by the classical physics, in which causality is perfectly obeyed and a state of perfect determinism exists, completely independent of any measuring apparatus or an observer; this is called entity *A*.

It may be noted that the assumption of this kind of reality or entity was considered to be irrelevant and physically meaningless by Heisenberg and others but it does not mean that they have completely ruled out the existence of this reality. This is because Heisenberg very clearly asserted that the laws of nature no longer deal with the nature itself but with the knowledge of the nature. Yet, it may also be worth mentioning that Einstein had a firm belief in the idea of the existence of a reality where the law of causality is perfectly obeyed and there is a state of perfect determinism, even after the discovery of quantum mechanics.

The second abstract entity, for which causality is neither obeyed nor violated, is called entity *B*. If we treat it as an abstract observer then the interrelation between these two entities *A* and *B* indicates that this new entity can be interpreted in two contradictory ways. According to one, the entity *B* is physically meaningless because it is void of any physical properties but according to the second interpretation, this new entity *B* can perceive the whole causal world in one single perception. The past, present and future of the causal world are perceived simultaneously.

This paradoxical situation appears to be very similar to the one described in Indian philosophy, whose main conclusion is that the true knowledge of this world is structured in the consciousness and hence can be obtained only through enlightenment, the complete detachment from the material world. It is argued that an enlightened consciousness is capable of perceiving the whole causal world in one perception from one point of view but from the other point of view this enlightened consciousness is a null, void of anything (Pokharna 2013a).

In connection to this, it is appropriate to mention Bohm (1980: 83-139, 177-99), who refers to perfect determinism within quantum mechanics through hidden variables with a defined implicate order, which is a deeper reality underneath the observable reality that is termed as explicate order. The state of implicate order is very similar to that of what a *kevala jñānī* perceives.

Free Will in Correlation to Multiple Dimensions of Time

In order to develop a "Theory of Everything" by including physics, philosophy, biological sciences, psychology and parapsychology, Neppe and Close (2012) have developed a nine-dimensional model of reality which includes three dimensions of space, three dimensions of time and three dimensions of consciousness. One-dimension is required to explain ordinary physical time; second dimension of time is required to explain phenomena like pre-recognition and a third dimension is required to explain free will in the domain of psychology. The physical time is directly related with determinism. Their work needs further studies in light of the issues pertaining to free will and complete determinism. It can provide an entirely new perspective to the matter of free will and determinism.

References

Ācārya Nanesh, 2008, *Jin Dhammo*, Bikaner: Akhil Bhartiya Sadhumargi Jain Shravak Sangh.

Animal Kill Counter, n.d., retrieved 18 August 2018, from Occupy for Animals: http://occupyforanimals.weebly.com/animal-kill-counter.html.

Bhandari, N., 2015, *Jainism: The Eternal and Universal Path to Enlightenment*, Jaipur: Prakrit Bharti Academy.

Bhandari, N. and S.S. Pokharna, 2017, "Syadavada and Anekantvada in the Modern Scientific Context", in *Compendium on Science and Mathematics in* Jainism, Ladnun, Rajasthan: Bhagawan Mahavir International Research Center for Scientific Research and Innovative Studies in Social Sciences.

Bohm, D., 1980, *Wholeness and the Implicate Order*, London: Routledge & Kegan Paul.

Buchanan, M., 2011, "Quantum Minds: Why We Think Like Quarks", *New Scientist*, 211(2828): 34-37.

Goldsmith, E., 1990, "Evolution, Neo-Darwinism and the Paradigm of Science", *The Ecologist*, 20(2): 67-73.

How Many Species We Are Losing? (2018, 15 December), retrieved 12 August 2019, from WWF: https://wwf.panda.org/discover/our_focus/biodiversity/biodiversity/

Kachhara, N.L., 2014, *Scientific Explorations of Jain Doctrine*, parts 1 & 2, Delhi: Motilal Banarsidass.

Kachhara, N.L., S.R. Tater and Samani U. Pragya, 2017, "Karma, Living Systems, Genes and Human Performance", in *Scientific Perspectives of Jainism*, ed. Samani C. Prajna, N.L. Kachhara and N. Bhandari, pp. 115-

49, Ladnun, Rajasthan: Bhagwan Mahaveer International Center for Scientific Research and Social Innovation Studies.

Knapton, S., 2014 (30 September), "Half of World's Animals Have Disappeared since 1970", *The Telegraph*, retrieved 30 July 2018, from https://www.telegraph.co.uk/news/earth/wildlife/11129163/Half-of-worlds-animals-have-disappeared-since-1970.html.

Kothari, D., 1985, "The Complementarity Principle and Eastern Philosophy", in *Neils Bohr: A Centenary Volume*, ed. A.P. Kennedy, pp. 325-31, Cambridge, MA: Harvard University Press.

Neppe, V.M. and E.R. Close, 2012, *Reality Begins with Consciousness: A Paradigm Shift That Works*, Washington, Brain Voyage.

Paulson, S., 2017 (4 May), *Roger Penrose on Why Consciousness Does Not Compute*, retrieved 18 June 2018, from Nautilus: https://nautil.us/issue/47/consciousness/roger-penrose-on-why-consciousness-does-not-compute.

Pokharna, S.S., 1985, "A New Investigation into the Problem of Perfect Determinism in Modern Science", *Indian Philosophical Quarterly*, XII(1): 67-84.

———, 2008, "Science Technology and New Paradigm of Philosophy: Modern Interpretation of Jain Philosophy", *Tirthankar Vani*, *8:* 53-58; 9: 59-62; 10: 59-61 & 11; and 12: 3-75.

———, 2013a, "Exploration of General Systems Theory and Jain Philosophy Could Provide New Ways of Looking at the Field of Bioethics", *Syntropy*, 2: 243-79, retrieved 24 August 2018, from http://www.sintropia.it/journal/english/2013-eng-2-18.pdf.

———, 2013b, "Limitations of Scientific Knowledge and the Concept of Knowledge through Consciousness in Jain Philosophy", *Journal of Gyan Sagar Science Foundation*, 1(1): 24-33.

———, 2015, "Quantum Field Theory, Consciousness and Jainism", *The International Journal for Transformation of Consciousness*, 1(1): 319-31.

Van Gigch, J.P., 1978, *Applied General Systems Theory*, New York: Harper and Row Publishers.

2

Determinism and the Karma Theory of Jainism

Prakash C. Kanthaliya

INDIAN philosophies share many concepts such as *dharma*, *karma*, reincarnation, suffering, renunciation and meditation, and almost all of them focus on the ultimate goal of liberation of the individual through diverse range of spiritual practices. They differ in their assumptions about the nature of existence as well as the specifics of the path to ultimate liberation, resulting in numerous schools of thought that disagree with each other. They are classified as orthodox (*āstika*) and heterodox (*nāstika*). Orthodox theories accept the authority of the Vedas, whereas the heterodox thought does not believe in the concept of the Vedas (Bowker 1997: 259; Doniger 2014: 46). There are six major schools of orthodox philosophy – Nyāya, Vaiśeṣika, Sāṁkhya, Yoga, Mīmāṁsā and Vedānta – and four major schools of heterodox philosophy – Jain, Buddhist, Ājīvika, Ajñāna and Cārvāka. All these schools of philosophy were formalized between 1,000 BCE to the early centuries of the Common Era.

The Śramaṇic movement before the sixth century BCE gave rise to a diverse range of heterodox beliefs, from accepting or denying the concept of soul, atomism, antinomian ethics, materialism, atheism, agnosticism, fatalism to free will, idealization of extreme asceticism to that of family life, strict *ahiṁsā* (non-violence) and vegetarianism to permissibility of violence and meat-eating. Notable philosophies that arose from the movement were Jainism, Buddhism, Cārvāka, Ajñāna and Ājīvika.

Cārvāka Philosophy

Cārvāka philosophy recognizes the direct evidence of materialistic life and does not accept the principle of supernatural power or God. Pleasure is the main objective of life which cannot be realized in the absence of sadness. The Cārvāka followers believe in eating, drinking and being merry. Those who do not enjoy the pleasures of life are considered to be stupid (Bhattacharya 2011: 166-67). Cārvāka philosophy does not believe that the soul is a separate entity. According to them, everything of the earth is made up of four elements, viz. earth, water, air and fire. The body is made by the special kind of combinations of these elements and creates consciousness which is called the soul. When the body gets destroyed, consciousness also ends. Cārvāka philosophy denies the existence of the metaphysical soul, heaven, hell and the theory of fatalism. Since Cārvākas do not believe in God and paradise, their philosophy is also called Lokāyata.

Ajñāna Philosophy

Ajñāna thought was the ancient school of radical Indian scepticism. It was a Śramaṇa movement and a major rival of early Buddhism and Jainism, and was also thus recorded in their texts. They held that it was impossible to obtain knowledge of metaphysical nature or ascertain the truth value of philosophical propositions; and even if knowledge was possible, it was useless and disadvantageous for final salvation (Jayatilleke 1963: 524). The Ajñāna believers claimed that the possibility of knowledge is doubtful since the claims to knowledge were mutually contradictory.

For example, sceptics assert that the soul is omnipresent and others say that it is not omnipresent. Some say that the soul is formless, while others say it is of the size of kernel of a grain of millet. Some say that it resides in heart and others say that it is located in the forehead. Therefore, Ajñāna followers believe that it is impossible to obtain complete knowledge of metaphysics.

There is no one with an outstanding intellect whose statement may be regarded as authoritative. Even if such a person exists, he cannot be discovered by limited knowledge. One who is not omniscient does not know everything, so how can one know that a certain person is omniscient? Without super knowledge, the knowledge of the means is not attained and, as a result, there is no attainment of the super knowledge of the object. This was the direct attack on those teachers who claimed themselves as omniscient, especially targeting the followers of Jainism, Buddhism, Pūrana Kassapa and Niyativāda.

Buddhist Philosophy

Buddhist philosophy started with the teachings of Siddhārtha Gautama and the Śramaṇa movement. Buddhism rejected the Vedic concept of *Brahman* (Ultimate Reality) and *ātman* (soul) philosophies of the Hindus. Buddhism shares many philosophical views with other Indian systems, such as belief in *karma* (cause and effect relationship), *saṁsāra* (ideas about cycle of life and rebirth), *dharma* (ideas about ethics, duties and values, permanence of all material things and body) and *nirvāṇa* or *mokṣa* (spiritual liberation). A major departure from Hindu and Jain philosophy in the Buddhist thought lies in the rejection of an eternal soul in favour of *anattā* (non-self) (Williams 2008: 96). *Anattā* is a composite Pāli word consisting of *an* (not, without) and *attā* (soul). The term refers that "there is in humans no permanent, underlying substance that can be called the soul". *Anattā* is synonymous with *anātman* (*an+ātman*) in Sanskrit Buddhist texts.

Ājīvika Philosophy

Ājīvika was the ancient school of Indian fatalism. It was a Śramaṇa movement and a major rival of early Buddhism and Jainism. The Ājīvika school of thought is known for Niyativāda (doctrine of absolute determinism). They believe that there is no free will and that everything that has happened, is happening and will happen is entirely pre-ordained in function of the cosmic principles.

Ājīvika metaphysics says that everything is composed of atoms and qualities emerging from aggregates of atoms. The aggregation and the nature of these atoms were predetermined by cosmic forces. Good and simple living is not a means to salvation but a means to true livelihood, predetermined profession and a way of life. All things are pre-ordained and therefore religion or ethical practice has no effect on one's future. People do things because cosmic principles make them do so and all that will happen is already predetermined (Barua 1920: 96). No human efforts could change *niyati* and *karma*, ethical theory, is a fallacy.

Yet, Ājīvika's belief in pre-determinism does not mean that they were pessimists. They simply did not believe in the moral forces of action. Action had immediate effects in one's current life but without any moral traces and both the action and the effect were predetermined.

Like Cārvākas, Ājīvikas were atheists and rejected the authority of the Vedas but unlike Cārvākas, they believed in everything there is an *ātman* – a central concept of Hinduism and Jainism. However, unlike Jains and various orthodox schools of Hinduism that held that the soul is formless, Ājīvikas asserted that the soul has a material form, one that helps meditation. They also believed that it passes through many births and ultimately progress into its pre-destined *nirvāṇa* (salvation).

Makkhali Gosāla, the propounder of the Ājīvika movement, seems to have combined the ideas of other schools of thought to form an eclectic doctrine (Basham 2002: 42-45). He appears to have believed in *niyati*, *svabhāva*, *saṅgati* and *pariṇāma*. According to him, all beings undergo development (*pariṇāma*). This culminates in the course of time into final salvation to which all beings are destined through factors of *niyati*, nature (*bhāva*) and change (*saṅgati*). As such, destiny does not appear as the only player but rather chance or indeterminism plays equal part in his doctrine. He, thus, subscribed to Niyativāda (fatalism) only in the sense that some future events, like salvation for all, were strictly determined.

Makkhali Gosāla

Makkhali Gosāla's mother and father were Bhadra and Maṅkhali, respectively. Gosāla's father was said to be employed as a *maṅkha*, a carrier of the image of a god or goddess who sang religious songs. Gosāla was so named because he was born in a cowshed, his parents being unable to find suitable lodgings in the village of Sarvana. Gosāla adopted his father's profession and become a *maṅkha* (Basham 2002: 35).

During the second year of Mahāvīra's asceticism, Gosāla came in contact with him in Nālandā. He was greatly attracted by Mahāvīra's penances and prayed to Mahāvīra to accept him a disciple but Mahāvīra did not entertain his request. He moved with Mahāvīra wherever he went and also practised penances. To test the knowledge of Mahāvīra, he asked about the receipt of *bhikṣā* during the Kārttika Pūrṇimā (full moon) festival. Gosāla was expecting a sweet at that celebration. Mahāvīra replied that he would not get that sweet. He would be served only by a sour desert and a useless coin. To prove him false, he started begging from morning and got nothing till evening. At the last he received a sour desert and a coin which later known as bad (Doshi 1977: 142-60). The incident led him to believe that whatever is to happen, will happen. Everything is predetermined and efforts do not make any differences. After that Gosāla shaved his head, threw his *citrapaṭṭa* and other equipment, as well as his clothes. He went to Mahāvīra who was staying in the outer area of Kollak village and prayed repeatedly to accept him as a disciple. Mahāvīra gave his approval.[1]

As Mahāvīra was going to Svarṇakhāla village with Gosāla, some cowmen were preparing puddings. Gosāla was very hungry and prayed to Mahāvīra that he would go there and eat puddings. Mahāvīra replied that cowmen would fail to prepare puddings and you would get nothing. Gosāla went to cowmen and said, "My *guru* has of all the three times knowledge and says that puddings will not be cooked." This really happened. The earthen pot broke down on having excess of rice. The cowmen ate the pudding each in broken pieces of earthen pot while Gosāla got nothing (*Āvaśyaka Cūrṇi* 283) (Doshi 1977: 142-60).

Several incidents in the narrative show that Mahāvīra made predictions that came true, despite Gosāla's repeated attempts to foil them. In one such incident, Gosāla asked Mahāvīra the fate of a sesame plant on seeing it by the roadside. Mahāvīra said that the plant would grow to fruition and the seed pod will grow into new plants. Determined to foil his *guru*'s prediction, Gosāla returned to the plant at night and uprooted it. Later, a sudden rain shower caused the plant to revive and reboot itself. Upon approaching the plant again later, Gosāla claimed to Mahāvīra that he would find his prophecy to have been foiled. Instead, he found the plant and its seed had developed exactly as predicted by Mahāvīra (*Āvaśyaka Cūrṇi* 283) (Basham 2002: 48-49). Gosāla was so impressed by the reanimation of the plant that he came to conclusion that man's efforts to change his destiny are futile as everything is predetermined. He developed the theory of Niyativāda. According to him, the soul's journey to salvation would take its own course and time. He believed in the cycle of births and rebirths and contended that this cycle is bound to go on to its destined course which cannot be changed by human efforts. As a result, all penances were found by him to be useless. He kept the company of Mahāvīra for about six years and then left.

---

1 *teṇaṁ ahaṁ goyamā* । *gosālassa maṅkhaliputtassa eyamaṭṭhaṁ paḍisuṇemi* ।।
– *Vyākhyāprajñapti* 15.44

Jain Theory of Karma

The *karma* theory of Jainism states that all the phenomena of the universe are linked together in the universal chain of cause and effect. No event can occur without definite cause behind it. The universe consists of six substances – *jīva, pudgala, dharma, adharma, ākāśa* and *kāla* which are held together by definite laws inherent in its own constitution. Although all six entities are eternal, they continuously undergo countless changes. During these transformations, nothing is created or destroyed. The universal law of cause and effect operates independently (Mehta 1998: 63-70).

According to Jain philosophy, every individual soul in pure state possesses infinite intuition, infinite knowledge, infinite power and infinite bliss.[2] All these attributes belong by nature to every soul in its perfection. Mundane souls are not perfect, because their knowledge and energy are found to be restricted. They are infected by foreign particles known as *karma. Kārmaṇa* particles are non-living matter and scattered all around us and all over the universe. A cluster of innumerable *kārmaṇa* particles is called *kārmaṇa vargaṇā.* Through the action of body, mind and speech, and acted upon anger, pride, deceit and greed, kārmic particles enter the soul and bind to it, the process is called as *bandha.*[3] The activities of thought, speech and body are responsible for the nature and quantity of the *karma-bandha.* The duration and intensity result from attachment and aversion.

The ignorant and deluded soul, bound with *karma*, continues to attract and bind new *karma* due to *kaṣāya* (passions) like anger, ego, deceit and greed. It is due to *karma* that the soul migrates from one life to another and passes through many pleasurable and painful situations. The ultimate goal for the soul is to achieve liberation from sufferings through understanding and realization

---

[2] *jñānadarśanadānalābhabhogopabhogavīryāṇi ca* । – *Tattvārthasūtra* 2.4

[3] *sakaṣāyatvājjīvaḥ karmaṇo yogyān pudgalānādatte* । *sa bandhaḥ* ।।
– Ibid. 8.2-3

of its intrinsic nature. Each living being is master of its own destiny. Salvation of the soul is possible by stopping influx of new *karma* and eliminating old ones.

At the time of bondage of *karmas* to the soul, four characteristics of *karmas* are decided:[4]

i. *Prakṛti* (*nature*): There are eight types of *karmas*. Depending upon the activities, one can accumulate one or more of these *karmas*: *jñānāvaraṇīya* (knowledge-obscuring *karma*), *darśanāvaraṇīya* (perception-obscuring *karma*), *mohanīya* (deluding *karma*), *antarāya* (energy-obscuring *karma*), *āyuṣya* (age-determining *karma*), *nāma* (body-determining *karma*), *gotra* (status-determining *karma*) and *vedanīya* (feeling-producing *karma*) (*Tattvārthasūtra* 8.5). These *karmas* are grouped into two categories: *ghātī karmas* (destructive) and *aghātī karmas* (non-destructive). *Ghātī karmas* destroy the true nature of the soul. *Aghātī karmas* do not destroy the nature of the soul, but affect the body in which the soul resides. The first four types of *karmas* are *ghātī karmas* and the last four are *aghātī karmas*.[5]

ii. *Pradeśa* (*quantity*): If the physical vigour of our activities is low, then we accumulate fewer *kārmaṇa* particles, but if the physical vigour is strong, then we accumulate larger numbers of *kārmaṇa* particles on our soul (*Tattvārthasūtra* 8.25).

iii. *Sthiti* (*duration*): The duration of the bondage of kārmic particles with the soul is decided by the intensity of our desires at the time of the activity. The milder the intensity, the shorter the duration of the *karman* bondage; the stronger the intensity, the longer the duration of bondage. The time

---

[4] *prakṛtisthityanubhāvapradeśāstadvidhayaḥ* । – *Tattvārthasūtra* 8.4

[5] *āvaraṇamohavigghaṁ ghādī jīvaguṇaghādaṇattādo* ।
āugaṇāṁ godaṁ veyaṇiyaṁ taha aghāditti ।।
– *Gommaṭasāra-Karmakāṇḍa* 9

that *karmas* stay bonded to the soul range from a fraction of a second to an innumerable number of years (*Tattvārthasūtra* 8.15-21).

iv. *Anubhāva* (*intensity*): The intensity of *karmas* depends upon how intense our passions are at the time of activities. The lesser the intensity of our passions, the less severe the resulting bondage; the greater the intensity, the more severe the resulting bondage (*Tattvārthasūtra* 8.22-23).

When *karmas* get attached to the soul, there are four levels of bondage (Jaini 1998: 112-113):

1. *Spr̥ṣṭa or śithila* (loose) *karmas* can be easily shed by regret;
2. *baddha or gadha* (tight) *karmas* can be shed by offering an apology;
3. *nidhatta* (tighter) *karmas* can be shed by very strong efforts, like austerity; and
4. *nikācita* (tightest) *karmas* can only be shed by bearing the results.

It should be realized that it is not always true that we have to wait in order to bear the results of our *karmas*; we can change the course of our *karmas* before they mature. It can be changed in duration and intensity, as well as in nature too in some cases. This is an important point because it means that not only we do have control over our *karmas*, but that we can change our fate.

Karmas obstruct these eight attributes of a pure soul (Mehta 1998: 190):

i. *Kevala jñāna* (perfect knowledge): State in which the soul knows everything, the past, present and future that is happening in the world, all at the same time. *Jñānāvaraṇīya karma* obscures this attribute.

ii. *Kevala darśana* (perfect perception): State in which the soul can see, hear and perceive everything from the past, present and future all at the same time. *Darśanāvaraṇīya karma* obscures this attribute.

iii. *Anantavīrya* (infinite power): State in which the soul has infinite power. *Antarāya karma* obstructs this attribute.

iv. *Vītarāga* (victory over inner enemies): State in which the pure soul has no attachment or hatred for anyone. *Mohanīya karma* obscures this attribute. Aforementioned four attributes of the soul are experienced by Lord *arihantas*.

The following four attributes are experienced only when the soul is liberated, when *arihantas* become *siddhas* upon their end of worldly life.

v. *Ananta ānanda* (infinite bliss/no joy or sorrow): State in which there is no suffering or happiness; the soul has ultimate peace. *Vedanīya karma* obscures this attribute.

vi. *Ajara-amara* (end of the cycle of birth and death): Point at which the soul is never again born. *Āyuṣya karma* obscures this attribute.

vii. *Arūpī* (no form): State in which the pure soul no longer occupies a body and is formless. *Nāma karma* obscures this attribute.

viii. *Agurulaghu* (end of status): Fact that all liberated souls are equal; none is higher or lower in status than any other. *Gotra karma* obscures this attribute.

Determinism and Jainism

The *karma* theory of Jainism rejects Niyativāda, but not in totality. Jain philosophy includes *niyati* as one of five essentials (*samavāyas*) that are present when any event occurs. These are:[6]

1. *Prakṛti* (nature): Establishes that the event would occur only if it is in the nature of the thing. For example, a statue cannot gain knowledge or a *jīva* cannot become insentient pot.

[6] *kālo sahāva niyaī puvvakayaṁ purise kāraṇeṅgatā* ı
micchattaṁ te ceva samāsao hoṁti sammattaṁ ıı
– *Sanmatitarka Prakaṇa* 3.53

2. *Nimitta* (catalyst): Describes that for every event to occur there may be numerous participating factors which apparently aid the event but in reality, they are just present. They do not contribute directly to the cause of the event but just denote the occurrence. That is why people confuse them as doer of the event.
3. *Puruṣārtha* (effort): Requires necessary effort on the part of the *jīva*, for any event to occur. Generally, people give very low importance to it and give credit to *nimitta*, but in reality, the event occurs because of effort. For example, a student passes an exam because of his effort to learn, although *nimitta* in the form of a teacher and books is present too.
4. *Kālalabdhi* (time for the event to occur): Recognizes that a certain time needs to elapse for an event to occur. For a student to pass an exam, a certain time should have elapsed in his life before which the event would not occur. When the time is ripe for the event, it occurs. This also explains why Mahāvīra was the 24th *tīrthaṅkara* while Ādinātha was the 1st in the current cycle of time.
5. *Niyati* (destiny): Defines the event *niyati* (destiny) defines that everything is pre-destined and whatever has to happen, good or bad, will happen. Contrarily whatever is not pre-destined to happen will never happen. All efforts to undo or oppose pre-destination will be in vain. For example, Mahāvīra became 24th *tīrthaṅkara* was the event which occurred at the appropriate time about 2,500 years back; it was not his destiny to be the first *tīrthaṅkara*.

Attainment of *mokṣa* occurs in *kālalabdhi* designated by *niyati*, by the destruction of *karmas* by *puruṣārtha*. Yet, certain questions can be raised in response to this; if it occurs by means of the first two *samavāyas*, then why do only a few of them make the effort even though all are being preached? The answer is that in occurrence of an event several essentials are present. For attainment of *mokṣa*, all essentials are present and for no attainment all the essentials are absent.

Time and destiny are not in our control. The *jīva* makes an effort to traverse the path of salvation and then other essentials also become present. If the *jīva* does not make efforts, then the presence of other essentials becomes irrelevant. *Karma*, which has been earned in the past, do bring fruit in the present life which cannot be avoided and one has to suffer. But even though one can mitigate the rigour by his own efforts, the *karma* theory believes that the future of a person depends upon good or bad deeds of the present.

The argument of some people who say that Jainism is Niyativāda is not correct. If we examine all the five essentials, we find that it is not only *niyati* but *puruṣārtha* as well as *nimitta*. When a thing has to happen, all would be seen to be present and when it does not occur all would be absent.

To summarize, it is stated that amongst the five factors which are equally important in the affairs of men (and all living beings), *puruṣārtha* is the first among the five equals. This leads to an optimistic approach and gives confidence to human beings, that they can mould their present and future as they will. This is true about matters that are temporal as well as spiritual. Indeed, many men have progressed on the spiritual path by the exercise of their will in the right manner. In matters of temporal nature, the progress made by men in scientific sphere is for everyone to see.

References

Ācārya Nemicandra, 1999, *Gommaṭasāra-Karmakāṇḍa*, ed. A.N. Shastri, New Delhi: Bharatiya Jnana pith.

Barua, B.M., 1920, *The Ajivikas*, Calcutta: University of Calcutta.

Basham, A.L., 2002, *History and Doctrines of the Ājīvikas: A Vanished Indian Religion*, Delhi: Motilal Banarsidass.

Bhattacharya, R., 2011, *Studies on the Cārvāka/Lokāyata*, London: Anthem Press.

Bowker, J., 1997, *Oxford Dictionary of World Religions*, Oxford: Oxford University Press.

Divākara, S., 1939, *Sanmati Tarka*, ed. D. Malvania, Bombay: Shri Jain Shwetambar Education Board.

Doniger, W., 2014, *On Hinduism*, Oxford: Oxford University Press.

Doshi, R.L., 1977, *Tīrthaṅkara Caritra*, vol. III: Sailana: Akhila Bhāratīya Sādhu Mārgī Jain Saṁskr̥ti Saṅgha.

Jaini, P.S., 1998, *The Jaina Path of Purification*, Delhi: Motital Banarsidass.

Jayatilleke, K., 1963, *Early Buddhist Theory of Knowledge*, London: George Allen and Unwin.

Madhukar Muni (ed.), 2003, *Vyākhyāprajñpti (Bhagavatī Sūtra)*, vol. III, Beawar: Shri Agam Prakashan Samiti.

Mehta, M.L., 1998, *Jain Philosophy: An Introduction*, Bangalore: Bharatiya Vidya Bhavan.

Surishwarji, A. (ed.), 2017, *Āvaśyaka Cūrṇi: Āvaśyaka Niryukti evaṁ Cūrṇi.* Paladi, Ahmedabad: Shri Param Anand Shwetambar Murtipujak Jain Sangh.

Umāsvāti, 2009, *Tattvārthasūtra*, ed. S. Sanghavi, Varanasi: Parshwanath Vidyapeeth.

Williams, P., 2008, *Mahayana Buddhism: The Doctrinal Foundations*, New York: Routledge.

3

Niyativāda in Jain Tradition

Shugan C. Jain

MAN is by nature inquisitive about himself and his environment. It leads him to enquire about the real, the unreal, the causes for events taking place around him, his control over them and whether he may be able to predict them.

Fatalism, determinism and pre-determinism are the terms generally used interchangeably in philosophical literature to stress different aspects of the futility of human will, or the fore-ordination of destiny.

Fatalism, termed Niyativāda in Sanskrit, stresses subjugation of all events or actions to fate. It implies that we are powerless to do anything other than what we actually do. Thus, a man has no power to influence the future, or indeed, his own actions. It results in an attitude of resignation in the face of future events which are thought to be inevitable.

However, Niyativāda should not to be confused with determinism, which implies that all events, including all choices made, are completely determined by previously existing causes. Determinism is usually understood to preclude free will because it entails that humans cannot act in another way than they do and, therefore, they cannot be held morally responsible for their actions. This leads one to become idle and leave everything to fate, as anticipated in *De Interpretatione* (Rice 2002). The theory holds that the universe is utterly rational because complete knowledge of any given situation assures that unerring knowledge of its future is also possible (based on cause and effect) (Wikipedia contributors 2021).

Determinism generally agrees that human actions affect the future but it is itself determined by a causal chain of prior events and, hence, they may subscribe to its being of probabilistic nature. Determinists believe the future is fixed by causality. However, causality can be of many types and affected by a vast number of independent actions. Their view does not accentuate a submission to fate, whereas fatalists stress an acceptance of future events as inevitable.

Jain Doctrine and Its Analysis

Jains are varyingly referred to as *Śramaṇas*, believers in self-effort to achieve self-reliance; *vrātyas*, one who observes vows, fasts; and *nigganthа*, without any possessions in Indian philosophical literature. They believe in the eternal existence of individual soul in each living being. The mundane soul is capable of attaining *mokṣa*, its pure soul state, through its own self-effort which is the ultimate objective of human life. Hence, whatever activity they partake in, they always keep their eyes on this objective. Thus, the nature of Jain doctrine itself refutes Jainism from supporting fatalism.

In the first three verses in the *Sūtrakr̥tāṅga*, Lord Mahāvīra discussed the doctrine of fatalists[1] and in verses

---

[1] Some say "It is proved that there are individual souls; they experience pleasure and pain; and (on dying) they lose their state of life. But misery (and pleasures) is not bound by (the souls) themselves; how could it be caused by others (agents like time)? Pleasure and misery, final beatitude and temporal (pain and pleasure) are not caused by (the souls) themselves, nor by others, but individual souls experience them; →

4-13,[2] he refuted their doctrine.

The extent to which fatalism is applicable in Jain philosophy will now be analysed.

Metaphysical Aspects of the Jain Doctrine of Reality

All beings (*vastu*) are real or existent. Even the phenomenal world is real and not an illusion. The Jain term for reality is *sat*. Reality is defined as "differentia of a substance" (*Tattvārthasūtra* 5.29), or the substance (*dravya*) is the differentia of reality or existence. Reality or substance is endowed with three characteristics, viz. origination, decay and permanence simultaneously.[3] Thus, a substance is not

← it is the lot assigned them by destiny". This is what they (the fatalists) say". – *Sūtṛakrtāṅga* 1.1.2.1

[2] Those, who proclaim these opinions, are fools who fancy themselves learned; they have no knowledge, and do not understand that things depend partly on fate, and partly on human exertion. Thus (say) some heretics; they are very bold men; if they act up to their principles, they will never be delivered from misery. As the swift deer who are destitute of protection, are frightened where there is no danger, and not frightened where there is danger. (As) they dread safe places, but do not dread traps; they are bewildered by ignorance and fear, and run hither and thither. If they did jump over the noose or pass under it, they would escape from the snare; but the stupid animal does not notice it. The unhappy animal, being of a weak intellect, runs into the dangerous (place), is caught in the snare and is killed there. So, some unworthy *Śramaṇas* who hold wrong doctrines are afraid of what is free from danger, and are not afraid of real dangers. The fools dread the preaching of the Law, but they do not dread works, being without discernment and knowledge. By shaking off greed, pride, deceit and wrath one becomes free from *karman*. This is a subject (which an ignorant man, like) a brute animal does not attend to. The unworthy heretics, who do acknowledge this, will incur death an endless number of times, like a deer caught in the snare/trap. –*Sūtrakṛtāṅga* 4-13

[3] *utpāda-vyaya-dhrauvya-yuktaṁ sat* । – *Tattvārthasūtra* 5.29

an inert entity as it keeps on transforming into different states, without the loss of its substantiality. In Jain philosophical terms, substance keeps on originating and decaying continuously from the mode viewpoint, while from the substance viewpoint, it always stays the same.

Another characteristic of *dravya* is that it is an amalgam of attributes (*guṇa*) and modes (*paryāya*) that exist simultaneously.[4] Those parts of the substance, which coexist with it, are the *guṇa* and those that occur serially (*krama*) are called the *paryāya*. Thus, substance is the base of both attributes and modes as these exist nowhere else except in the substance. There are two types of attributes: generic ones which are present in all substances that never get changed or eliminated, and specific ones to a grouping of substances whose status keeps on transforming. The state of transformation of attributes of a substance at any time instant is *artha paryāya*. The series of instant modes are called *vyañjana paryāya* – a set of instant transformations. There are many other classifications of modes on similar lines as well.

Dualism

All existents are classified into two categories, viz. those with consciousness and its manifestation called *jīva*, living beings; and those without consciousness called *ajīva*, non-living beings. *Jīva* is the agent of its *karmas* and the enjoyer of their fruits. *Jīva* is of the same size of the body it owns and has the nature to move upwards (*Dravyasaṁgraha* 1-10). Similarly, *ajīva* is divided into two categories, viz. active and perceptible called *pudgala* (matter) and inactive and supporting the activities of *jīva* and *pudgala*. The inactive *ajīva* substances are further subdivided as principles of motion (*dharma*), rest (*adharma*), space (*ākāśa*) and the change associated with the passage of time (*kāla*) (*Tattvārthasūtra* 5.17-18, 22). Matter is active with fusion and fission as its nature is with randomness of

---

[4] *guṇa-paryāyavad-dravyaṁ* । – Ibid. 5.38

its activities. *Jīva* and *pudgala* can be further subdivided into many subcategories. For instance, *jīva* is categorized as the pure soul (*siddha*) and the empirical soul or embodied soul.

Saṁsāra

The animation/activity of the *jīva*[5] and its interactions with *pudgala* are represented by seven verities (*tattvas*) of their existence in the world and is termed as *saṁsāra*. These *tattvas* are *jīva*, *ajīva*, *āsrava*, *bandha*, *saṁvara*, *nirjarā* and *mokṣa* (*Tattvārthasūtra* 1.4). *Jīva* is an amalgam of soul and matter in the form of *karmas* and bodies of different types. When *jīva*'s association with matter is completely eliminated, *jīva* has attained the state of *mokṣa*. On the other hand, *pudgala* with its inherent nature of fusion and fission keeps on interacting with *jīva* or with other forms of *pudgala* aggregates to give different perceptible objects in this world.

Jīva

Every *jīva* wants to be happy, with the ultimate goal to attain the state of bliss and pure knowledge. *Jīva* is active and endowed with the choice of one of the five dispositions (*Tattvārthasūtra* 2.1), termed as free will (*upayoga*) when faced with the rise of *karmas* bonded with it. Thus, *jīva* (soul) is the material cause while all other numerous external causes are considered as efficient causes that are likely to affect the *upayoga* of *jīva*. Further classification of *jīvas* as *bhavya* and *abhavya* adds to the complexities of our analysis of free will (*Sarvārthasiddhi* 2.7.268). Similarly, the classification of one to five sensed living beings and the bondage or annihilation of *karmas* specific to some of the four destinies (human, subhuman, hell and heaven) add to the discussions about the exercise of free will by *jīvas*.

Jain Metaphysics

The definition of the reality of substance indicates as with

---

[5] *upayogo lakṣanaṁ* – *Tattvārthasūtra* 2.8.

simultaneous the notion of origination-destruction and permanence that it is both permanent and impermanent as its inherent nature leads to analyse the characteristics and existence of each existent from two viewpoints: from permanence of substance viewpoint and from impermanence of modal viewpoint. Thus, all substances from substance viewpoint can be said to endorse Niyativāda when they are not associated with other substances of the same category.

In the case of *jīva* as an empirical soul (*saṁsārī jīva*), it is different. The *saṁsāri jīva* is a blend of pure soul which is immaterial plus matter bodies classified as physical (*audārika* or *vaikriyaka*), *kārmica* and luminary (*tejas*). Both soul and *pudgala* are active substance types and hence they affect each other's *paryāya* as indicated by the *tattvas* and nine entities (*padārthas*).[6]

The physical body is a mechanical collection of a large number of interconnected matter parts whose behaviour is well documented in Jain literature, primarily as ninety-three variants of *nāma-karma*, as well as in biology and medical science with a cause and effect relation. Jainism (*Dravyasaṁgraha* 1-10), however, considers each matter part of the body to be associated with its counterpsychic part as well (soul is coexistent with the body it owns) to impart consciousness in them that further enables them to interact with external environment as well as within the body itself. So, the functioning of the material body is partly predictable like a mechanical clock at all places and partly different like microprocessor-based clocks in smart phones which adjust according to the place where it is in the world. Kārmic activities will be discussed separately later.

---

[6] (a) *bhūdattheṇābhigadā jīvājīvā ya puṇṇapāvaṁ ca* ।
āsavasaṁvaraṇijjarabandhomokkho ya sammataṁ ।।
– *Samayasāra* 1.13

(b) *ṇava ya padatthā jīvājīvā tāṇaṁ ca puṇṇapāvadugaṁ* ।
āsavasaṁvaraṇijjarabandhāmokkho ya hoṁtitti ।।
– *Gommaṭasāra-Jīvakāṇḍa* II.621

By definition, *paryāyas* are an unbroken series of origination and destruction of instant states of a quality occurring serially; yet the direction of the series of modes can be affected by two types of causes: material (*upādāna*) caused by the *jīva* and efficient (*nimitta*) caused by others. Siddhasena Divākara talks of five cofactors (*samvāyas*) to explain the rise of a new mode/event in such cases:

> *kālo sahāvo niyai puvvakayaṁ purise kāraṇogatā* ।
> *micchattaṁ te ceva u, samāsao honti sammattaṁ* ॥
> – *Sanmatitarka Prakaraṇa* 3.53

> Time (*kāla*), nature (*svabhāva*), universal laws (*niyati*), pre-executed *karmas*, and self-effort (*puruṣārtha*) are the five co-factors which explain an event; consideration of any one in isolation is absolutism (*mithyā*).

Niyati or *bhāgya* are translated as fate or pre-ordained, while others define it as universal laws (setting limits to the cause and effect relation) and is more appropriate. Either way, it is one of the factors thereby indicating that just supporting *niyati* is *mithyā*. This seems to be in line with René Descartes (duality of existence), though going further to identify even the material world differently. Thomas Nagel, who moved further in his analysis, comes closer to the Jain analysis above.[7] Even though Jains claim that the process of events

---

[7] In 2012, Thomas Nagel proposed an account of evolution that incorporates impersonal, natural teleological laws to explain the existence of life, consciousness, rationality and objective value. He says, "The message is that there is a limit to the extent to which we can 'get outside' fundamental forms of thought, including logical, mathematical, scientific and ethical thought. Getting outside means ourselves as thinkers and taking up a biological or psychological, or sociological or economic or political view of the world." He ends by saying, "Even if we distance ourselves from some of our thoughts and impulses, and regard them from outside, the process of trying to place ourselves in the world leads eventually to thoughts that we cannot think of as merely 'ours' ". – Blackburn n.d.

expressed as series of modes tightly interlinked looks to support the mechanistic view, they talk, like Nagel, of a number of external causes which can and do affect the direction in which the series of modes proceeds.

There is also a corpus of scholarly analyses in the twentieth century, like that of Hukam C. Bharil, on *kramabaddha paryāya*,[8] where *baddha* means bound by a system of definite occurrences as a rule in a particular fashion. This analysis presumes that efficient causes such as effort, time, nature and environmental conditions will continue to be the same or are exactly predicable. For these analyses, they depend heavily on the concept of the omniscient human being (*sarvajña*), who knows each and every state of all substances of the past, present and future.[9] To support these statements, he relies heavily on the concept of no changes in intrinsic and extrinsic nature of *jīva*. The concept of *siddhas* or the soul itself, identified as *svasamaya* by Kundakunda (*Samayasāra* 1.2), in *guṇasthānas* 13th and 14th does support this, as its intrinsic and extrinsic nature is always same. This paper, however, discusses the state of empirical souls (*parasamaya*) only (*guṇasthānas* from 1st up to 12th).

This leads to the conclusion that the future state of an empirical

---

[8] "A specific *paryāya* [mode] of that specific substance is to take place in that particular *kṣetra* [place], in that particular *samay* [time], in the presence of that specific *nimitta*, with the specific *purushartha*, in that particular fashion; the very same specific *paryay* [mode] of that very specific substance does take place in that very specific *kshetra* [area], in that particular *samay* [time], in the presence of that very specific *nimitta*, with that very specific *purushartha* and exactly in that particular fashion; And in none other way." – Shah 2002: 123

[9] Even though an omniscient knows everything of past, present and future, he never speaks or writes. It is the other non-omniscient persons who interpret his knowledge and the same is further complicated as the exact written details for the same are not available today.

soul is not just predicable as per Niyativāda, as a large number of intrinsic and extrinsic causes affect the same.

When a *karma* bonded to the empirical soul becomes active or starts yielding fruits, the *bhāva*, that is a characteristic of a soul can manifest in one of the five ways,[10] viz. to enjoy its inherent nature (*pāriṇāmika*), to be at the mercy of *karmas* (*udaya*), to try to suppress *karmas* (*upaśama*), to destroy (*kṣaya*) them or to both suppress and destroy (*kṣayopaśamika*) them, making it difficult to explain the end result of series of modes even though all activities of soul are purposive. However, the deluding *karma* and its potency causes its unpredictable actions, even though the *jīva* is said to be the doer of matter *karmas*, while the pure soul is the doer and enjoyer of *bhāva karmas* (psychic actions) and its own nature. Human conduct, insofar as it is rational, is generally explained with reference to the ends or goals pursued or alleged, either intrinsic, the nature to be happy and achieve bliss, or extrinsic, like to be loved and respected by others.

On its own, *pudgala* acts randomly. One category of *pudgala* that is of use to the *jīva* is called *vargaṇās*. Other forms of *pudgala* can be influenced by *jīva* to generate specific objective-oriented entities that support teleology generally. However, the complexity of the likely influences of other matter and *jīva*[11] tends to make predictions that do not support Niyativāda.

Karma Doctrine of Jainism

Karma in Jain doctrine consists of subtle matter particles associated with soul. These *karma* particles store the actions performed by *jīva* along with the likely results, their nature, duration and time of fructifying. These *karma* particles are self-accentuated thereby meaning no divine intervention in their effect. Thus, it seems

---

[10] *aupaśamikakṣāyikaubhāvaumiśraśca jīvasya svatattvamaudayikapāriṇāmikau ca* । – *Tattvārthasūtra* 2.1

[11] *parasparopagraho jīvānāṁ* । – Ibid. 5.21

that *karma* doctrine of Jains support the cause-effect relationship largely. However, a detailed analysis of the *karma* doctrine shows something else.

Karmas are divided into two categories: obscuring (affect the nature of pure soul) and non-obscuring (do not affect the nature of pure soul but are experienced by *jīva*).[12] Each is further subdivided into four subtypes for a total of 148 sub-sub-types. Deluding *karma*, the most potent obscuring *karma* affects the nature and results of all other *karmas*. Some important considerations in *karma* are:

i. Disposition (and its type) of soul has different effects on the *karmas*. Thus, free will comes into play. *Guṇasthānas* depict clearly the effect of dispositions and the deluding *karmas* abundantly.

ii. Some *karmas* only, like *tīrthaṅkaranāma karma* and *āyu karma* once bound with the soul, cannot be changed.

iii. *Karmas* can exist in one of ten states. Almost all states can be changed by exercising free will and self-effort except one state called *nikācita*.

iv. The ultimate objective of soul is to extinguish all *karmas* and be *asiddha*.

Thus, it seems that the *karma* doctrine, even though based on the direct cause and effect relationship, cannot just support Niyativāda.

Jain Ethics and Fatalism

Jains have moral rules in the form of vows like *aṇuvratas* and *mahāvratas*, *gūṇavratas* and *śikṣāvratas*. They talk of every action to be judged on the goodness of the consequences expected. However, it is difficult to calculate the consequences of each and every action as it accepts the possibility of general moral principles being

---

[12] *āvaraṇamohaviggham ghādī jīvaguṇaghādaṇattādo* ı
āugaṇāṁgodaṁ veyaṇiyaṁ taha aghāditti ıı – *Gommaṭasāra-Karmakāṇḍa* 9

inadequate to the complexities of the situation. Accordingly, Jain ethics talk of flaws of the vows and their correction in the form of *pratikramaṇa* (repentance). *Tattvas* like influx, stoppage, bondage and dissociation show these effects.

Furthermore, Jain ethics suggest that acts are logically prior to rules and the rightness of the action is situational. Jain ethics support that right and duty cannot be separated from the good (Sogani 2013: 200). The equivalent expression in Jain ethics for the term "right" and "good" is *śubha*. It explains how to determine, according to Jainism, what is morally right for a certain agent in a certain situation. Or what the criterion of the rightness of action is. The Jain ethics hold the teleological theory of right (maximum balance of *ahiṁsā* over *hiṁsā* as the right-making characteristic), that is the goodness of the consequences of actions as the right-making characteristic.

In Jain ethics, duty is not self-justifying, an end in itself. There can no more be a duty to act, if there is no good to attain by it. Thus, duty is an extrinsic good as a means without depriving duty of its importance in ethical life. The intrinsically desirable, i.e. *śubha*, is: what ought to be chosen for its own sake is the achievement of *ahiṁsā* of all living beings and the attainment of knowledge. Thus, *śubha* is an experience in tune with *ahiṁsā*. It basically embraces all the aspects of social experience in its normative perspective.

Normative Aspects of Jainism, Historical Literature and Fatalism

All universal laws supporting Niyativāda are generally derived from the historical and mythical literature of Jainism, such as the twenty-four *tīrthaṅkaras* only occurring in the fourth *ārā* of an epoch and their predictability by an omniscient; the sixty-three illustrious persons only including *tīrthaṅkaras* in an epoch; the 108 *jīvas* from *nigoda* get out in six months and eight time-instants (*samaya*) and the equal number attain liberation; the five auspicious events in the life of a *tīrthaṅkara*. All these references imply a set of rules, like *vratas* in Jain ethics; however, their implications in specific cases are situational.

As Jain doctrine promotes *anekānta* (non-absolutism) as the basis of our acquiring right knowledge. Thus, the definition of real as existent with persistence and change leads one to look at an entity from at least two viewpoints; permanence or substance viewpoint, as well as from impermanence or mode viewpoint. Accordingly, we conclude that the likely state, both from the substance viewpoint and the modal viewpoint of the *jīva* and their associated events, will be as follows:

i. *Pure soul*: The soul after liberation, continues to enjoy its own inherent nature forever. Hence, all its future states are fully predictable and support Niyativāda.

ii. *Empirical soul*: The pure soul amalgamated with matter in the form of kārmic, physical body, is affected both by its intrinsic and extrinsic nature. Therefore, its future states cannot be predicted fully and do not support Niyativāda.

References

Ācārya Kundakunda, 2012, *Samayasāra*, ed. V.K. Jain, Dehradun: Vikalp Printers.

Ācārya Nemicandra, 2000, *Gommaṭasāra-Jīvakāṇḍa*, ed. A.N. Shastri, New Delhi: Bharatiya Jnanpith.

———, 2010, *Dravyasaṅgraha*, tr. N. Balbir, Mumbai: Hindi Granth Karyalaya.

Ācārya Pūjyapāda, 1997, *Sarvārthasiddhi*, ed. P. Shastri, New Delhi: Bharatiya Jnanpith.

Blackburn, S., n.d., *Review of Thomas Nag=el: The Last Word*, Retrieved 30 January 2018, from Faculty of Philosophy: http://www2.phil.cam.ac.uk/~swb24/reviews/Nagel.htm.

Diwakara, S., 1939, *Sanmati Tarka*, ed. D. Malvania, Bombay: Shri Jain Shwetambar Education Board.

Rice, H., 2002 (18 December), *Fatalism*, retrieved 24 August 2018, from

Stanford Encyclopedia of Philosophy: https://plato.stanford.edu/entries/fatalism/.

Shah, U.D., 2002, *Karan Karya Rahasya*, ed. M.R. Shah, Mumbai: Veetragvani Prakashak.

Sogani, K.C., 2013, "Religion and Morality (Ethics): Jaina Perspective", in *Study Notes (Selected Papers on Jainism)*, vol. II, pp. 195-202, New Delhi: International School for Jain Studies.

Sūtrakṛtāṅga-Jaina Sūtra, Part II, 1996, tr. H. Jacoby, Delhi: Low Price Publications.

Umāsvami, 2011, *Tattvārthasūtra*, ed. V.K. Jain, Dehradun: Vikalp Printers.

Wikipedia contributors, 2021 (13 April) *Determinism*, retrieved 15 April 2021, from Wikipedia, The Free Encyclopedia: https://en.wikipedia.org/wiki/Determinism

4

Free Will in Jainism

Christopher K. Chapple

THE earliest extant text of the Jain tradition, the *Ācārāṅgasūtra*, espouses adherence to vows as the primary way of achieving the intended spiritual goals of the tradition. This text, dating from 300 BCE, is accepted by the adherents to the Śvetāmbara or white-clad group of Jains, but rejected by the other main group of Jains, the Digambara or sky-clad. Both agree on a later text, the *Tattvārthasūtra* of Umāsvāti, thought to have been composed in 5 CE. This text expounds on the foundational principles of Jain belief, particularly its description of the soul (*jīva*), how it becomes sullied through self-effort with *karma* and how it can be purified and set free from kārmic bondage. Literature from each tradition will be considered on the topic of will, including the *Yogadṛṣṭisamuccaya* of Haribhadra (eighth century Śvetāmbara) and the *Pravacanasāra* and *Samayasāra* of Kundakunda (*c.* fifth century Digambara). This paper also examines the positions found in the *Samaṇa Suttam*, a twentieth-century text accepted by both traditions and some contemporary field research will also be cited.

Jainism, like Buddhism and Yoga tradition, emphasizes kārmic causality in its philosophy. It does not posit a creator deity such as Brahmā or Prajāpati, nor does it advance the notion of an originating matrix such as *prakṛti*. The Jain world view asserts the existence of innumerable souls (*jīvas*) that become obscured by their *karmas*. These *karmas*, like the *jīvas* themselves, are particular and individual. The path of Jain purification requires that they be expelled or extirpated through assiduously adhering to strict ethical rules. By sloughing off these *karmas*, one attains increasingly rarefied spiritual states. Ultimately, this process culminates in the liberation and the ascent of the undying, conscious soul to a beatific state. According to the system, will reigns supreme. Through acts of will vitiated by violent intent, *karmas* adhere to the soul. Through acts of will inspired by a desire to do no harm, *karmas* fly away, leaving the soul lighter and less burdened and ultimately free to soar into endless energy, consciousness and bliss.

The Ācārāṅgasūtra

Jainism traces its origins back to the teacher Pārśvanātha, who lived approximately in 850 BCE, in north-east India. Three to four hundred years later, Mahāvīra codified the teachings of Pārśvanātha. These two religious leaders are considered within the Jain tradition to be the 23rd and 24th of a long line of liberated guides known as *tīrthaṅkaras*, or those who have forded the stream. This epithet indicates that these great *jina* victors have conquered the stream of *karma* and reached the banks of the other shore of liberation. From their place of splendid luminosity, they dwell in perpetual consciousness, energy and bliss, perched atop their own mountain, endlessly surveying the play of *karma* below. The singular, heroic nature of this achievement is qualified as *kevala* – simple, pure, uncompounded, unmingled, entire, whole, all (Monier-Williams 1899: 310).

From the onset, the *Ācārāṅgasūtra* sets forth a voluntarist view. It begins with an exhortation to know one's orientation within the four cardinal directions and to accept the premise that the "soul is born again and again. The opening passage goes on to state that a Jain believes in soul, believes in the world, believes in reward and believes in action to be of our own doing in judgments such as: "I did it", "I shall cause another to do it" and "I shall allow another to do it". In the world, these are all the causes of sin which must be comprehended and renounced" (*Ācārāṅgasūtra* 1.1.1.5).

The translator adeptly points out that the belief in a soul sets Jainism apart from the materialist Cārvākins, that the reference to the reality of the world distinguishes the Jains from the Vedāntins, and that the cause of all suffering lies in action (*kriyā*). Jains, unlike the Cārvākas, teach the existence of a soul. Unlike the Vedāntins, they teach that each soul remains individual and that the world is real. Jains consider the difficulties encountered to be an incentive toward self-improvement by performing a pure action, the soul purifies itself.

The commitment to non-violent action defines Jainism. Acts of non-violence are intentionally undertaken. The *Ācārāṅgasūtra* (1.2.3.3) states:

> A wise man should neither himself commit violence ..., nor order others to commit violence ..., nor consent to the violence done by somebody else.

The text repeatedly extols penance, self-restraint and control as the means of purification. It also lauds the Jain practitioner as a hero:

> *The hero should conquer wrath and pride,*
>
> ....
>
> *Here now the hero, knowing bondage,*
> *Knowing sorrow, should restraint himself.*
> *Having risen to birth among men,*
> *He should not take the life of living beings.* – Ibid. 1.3.3

The use of the term "conquer" plays a pre-eminent role in the text, with regard to conquering negative actions (*karmas*) such as "wrath, pride, deceit and greed." – Ibid. 1.3.4.1

It is important to note that this effort is not exerted to create or engage in worldly activities, but to purge oneself of *karmas* that bind one to the cycle of birth, life, death and rebirth. The goal is to assiduously follow Jain precepts that protect all forms of life, not necessarily for their sakes, but to purify oneself of kārmic accretions. The meticulous articulation of the places that contain life requires utmost attentiveness. The *Ācārāṅgasūtra* begins with a thorough analysis of the elemental presences of life before turning to the more obvious presence of life in vegetation, in bacteria and in animals. Hence, the Jain monk is advised to be vigilant not to commit harm to earth bodies, water bodies, as well as the forms of life in fire and air. The following passage conveys a sense of the care to be observed:

> There are beings living in the earth, living in grass, living on leaves, living in wood, living in cow dung, living in dust-heaps, jumping beings which coming near (fire) fall into it. Some certainly, touched by fire, shrivel up; those which shrivel up there, lose their sense there; those which lose their sense there, die there.
>
> ... a wise person should not act sinfully towards fire, nor cause others to do so, nor allow others to do so. He who knows the causes of sin relating to fire is called a reward-knowing sage ... .
>
> – *Ācārāṅgasūtra* 1.1.4.6-7

The text goes on to itemize the eight ways in which life takes form, including from eggs, from a foetus, from fluids (worms), from sweat (lice), from coagulation (locusts, ants), from sprouts (butterflies) and by regeneration (animals, humans, gods, hell-beings) (ibid. 1.1.6.1).

Punishments due to past action can be severe. The *Ācārāṅgasūtra* 1.6.1.3 attributes such problems as boils and leprosy, consumption, sickness, blindness and stiffness, lameness and being hump-backed, dropsy and dumbness, epilepsy, eye disease, trembling and being crippled, elephantiasis and diabetes to the fruits of their own acts. In order to rid oneself of the afflictions that cause such unpleasant experiences, Mahāvīra urges taking up the monastic life. Practising these austerities, the monk or nun, "neither injuring nor injured, becomes a shelter for all sorts of afflicted creatures, even as an island, which is never covered with water" (ibid. 1.6.5.4). Detailed rules are given that govern the life of monks and nuns, specifying that one may own at most only three robes and one begging bowl and a perhaps a broom. The ideal observance of male monasticism includes the option of total nudity and renunciation of even the begging bowl (ibid. 1.7.7.1-3). Enduring great hardship and discomfort, including reviling blows from non-believers, the monk or nun bears the pains caused by grass, cold, fire, flies and gnats; and he/she uses miserable beds and miserable seats, as did Mahāvīra (ibid. 1.8.3.1-2).

The second book of the *Ācārāṅgasūtra* expands the list of ways in which the Jain monk or nun must exert his or her will in order to best adhere to the precepts of the faith, including how and where and when to beg for food, the requirement that one avoid various specific forms of entertainment or festivals that might stir the passions, and that they should not point accusingly at anyone. Detailed lists are provided regarding unacceptable food, including bulbous roots, ginger, raw mango, unripe wild rice, honey, liquor, ghee and many others (ibid. 2.1.8.3-8). Places to avoid lodging include those

> used by the householder, in which there are women, children, cattle, food and drink. A mendicant, who lives together with a householder's family, may have an attack of gout, dysentery, or vomiting; or some other pain, illness, or disease may befall him.
>
> – Ibid. 2.2.1.8

Monks also avoid living with householders because they may become sexually aroused by "the householder's wives, daughters, daughters-in-law, nurses, slave-girls or servant girls" (ibid. 2.2.1.12). Monks and nuns are restricted from travelling in the rainy season due to potential harm caused to living beings such as insects. They must take care to avoid thieves, guard their speech and avoid acquiring anything beyond essential clothing. The purification practices observed increase the *tapas* (spiritual heat) of the monks and nuns. The text concludes with a summary account of the life of Mahāvīra, the exemplar for adherents to the faith.

In reading the *Ācārāṅgasūtra*, one finds not only a philosophy and a way of life based on voluntary action, but also exhaustive and somewhat exhausting detail in regard to behaviours to be avoided and behaviours to be cultivated.

The Tattvārthasūtra

Earlier Prākṛt texts such as the *Ācārāṅgasūtra* and the *Kalpasūtra* provide narrative accounts of how best to practise the Jain faith, whereas the fifth century *Tattvārthasūtra* falls within the genre of Sanskrit philosophical texts that set forth premises and assertions, that gives the reader a comprehensive world view that leads them to religious practice, culminating in freedom. Cosmology leads to insight; insight leads to religious commitment; religious commitment delivers one into a life of purified action and ultimately freedom. Authored by the scholar Umāsvāti, this text has earned acceptance from both sects of Jainism – Śvetāmbaras and Digambaras – who have disagreed on many other issues since their separation, most likely due to famine, 2,300 years ago. They disagree on the details of Mahāvīra's biography and on the potential spiritual status of women (Śvetāmbaras proclaim that women can attain release; Digambaras say that they need to reincarnate as a man to do so), but they agree on the principles set forth by Umāsvāti: *karma* causes rebirth, vows cleanse one of *karma*; through diligent adherence to Jain vows, one can purge *karma* and gain release.

Umāsvāti composed ten chapters that describe the progression from cosmology to *karma*, to ethics and finally to liberation. The first chapter includes a summary view of Jainism that reveals its fundamental commitment to a philosophy of free will. It works with an ascending hierarchy of three binaries leading to liberation, contrasting soul with matter and contrasting the inflow and binding of *karma* with the stoppage and expulsion of *karma*, resulting in "liberation from worldly (kārmic) bondage" (*Tattvārthasūtra* 1.4). Each soul authors its own existence, inviting *karma* to stick to its visage through the performance of action.

Souls and matter have always existed. Jainism does not allow for the presence of creator deity. Individuals create themselves in their present state, generally sullied with the presence of kārmic matter. *Karmas* flow onto the soul, sticking to it and shrouding the soul with tendencies and predispositions. Through taking up the religious life, one is able to first stop the influx of more *karma* and gradually slough off the *karmas* that have accrued over time. Though the stories of great heroic spiritual teachers, such as Mahāvīra, may inspire an individual to be steady in his or her religious practice, each soul creates and follows their own solitary destiny. Vows must be observed and performed from within; no god, demon or human being can affect adherence to or straying from the commitment to expel all the fettering *karmas* from one's soul.

In the second chapter of the *Tattvārthasūtra* (2.1), Umāsvāti describes the eight forms of *karma* that shape reality: knowledge-covering; intuition-covering; sensation-covering; deluding; lifespan-determining; body-making; status-determining; obstructive. Details follow that describe all the various forms of life that falls way to the influences of these *karmas*, divided into mobile and non-mobile forms. Unlike Aristotle, who defined life in terms of respiration and growth, Umāsvāti, following the ideas of earlier Jain teachers such as Mahāvīra in the *Ācārāṅgasūtra* as mentioned above, sees life in earth particles, water drops, flickering flames and gusts of wind. To each life form is attributed at least one sense. Souls trapped by *karma* in the form of earth or plants possess the consciousness of touch. Worms and leeches add taste, bugs add smell, flying insects add sight, and larger beings including fish, mammals humans and gods add hearing and mind.

The text delineates three domains: the infernal regions, the middle realm of earth and the heavenly region. The liberated soul can only attain release from containment in these zones into a place of liberation known as the *siddhaloka* by attaining human birth and then entering and completing the Jain path of purification. Chapter three details the lower and middle region, comprising a remarkable geography interwoven with moral implications. If one performs evil actions, one descends into the various hells. On earth, known as Jambūdvīpa, elements, plants, as well as non-human animals are given the opportunity to cultivate virtue.

The heavenly realm, described in chapter four, includes many varieties of gods and goddesses. In the lower realms of heaven, they enjoy sexual activity, while in the higher realms they find sexual pleasure through sight, sound and thought (ibid. 4.8-10). Ten "mansion gods" are listed as follows:

> fiendish youths, serpentine youths, lightning youths, vulturine youths, fiery youths, stormy youths, thundering youths, oceanic youths, island youths, and youths who rule the cardinal points.
>
> – Ibid. 4.11

Other types of gods include forest gods and luminous gods, located in more than two dozen heavens. One could psycho-analyse these various beings related to their realms. The descriptions indicate that one "earns" status due to past action. Furthermore, these domains are not destinations but way stations; in order to advance toward freedom, each soul must reinhabit human form.

The fifth chapter describes substances, considering the soul and *karma* alike to be substantial. It additionally names categories that are non-sentient: matter, motion, rest and space. Soul has consciousness; matter, motion, rest and space have no consciousness. Within this amalgam of ingredients, reality takes form as individual consciousnesses that interact with the material environment. According to the commentaries, vibrations (*spanda*) of the soul attract particular forms of *karma*, that fall into the eight types of reality-shaping *karmas*. The sixth chapter specifies: "[g]ood actions cause the inflow of beneficial *karma*. Evil actions cause the inflow of harmful *karma*" (ibid. 6.3-4). The commentary gives details of the various forms of *karma*, such as the five senses, the four passions (anger, pride, deceit and greed), the five indulgences (causing harm, lying, stealing, licentiousness and possessiveness) and the twenty-five urges:

1. urges that lead to enlightened world view,
2. urges that lead to deluded world view,
3. evil urges of body, speech and mind,
4. the inclination of the ascetic to abstain,
5. urges that produce instantaneous inflow,
6. physical enthusiasm,
7. using instruments of destruction,
8. malicious activity,
9. torturous activity,
10. murderous activity,
11. urges for visual gratification,
12. urges for tactile,
13. inventing and manufacturing lethal weapons,
14. evacuating bowels or vomiting at gatherings of men and women,
15. occupying uninspected and unswept places and living things there,
16. undertaking others' duties out of anger or conceit,
17. approving of an evil act,
18. divulging the sins of others,
19. arbitrary interpretation of scriptural teachings,
20. disrespect for the scriptural teachings,

21. damage to the environment such as digging earth, tearing leaves, etc.
22. possessive clinging,
23. deceitful actions,
24. promotion of deluded views, and
25. harbouring passions and possessiveness).

The first five urges provide a roadmap to understanding human will. The assessment of the innate human condition is actually quite grim. Only the first urge leads to the enlightened world view. The other twenty-four urges cause delusion, various forms of evil, malicious, torturous and murderous activities, disrespect for scriptural teachings and more (ibid. 6.6).

The *Tattvārthasūtra* specifies the causes that inhibit consciousness:

> Slander, concealment, envy, obstructiveness and disregard or condemnation of the scripture, its keepers and instruments, cause the inflow of knowledge-covering and intuition-covering *karmas*. Causing pain, grief, agony, crying, injuring or lamenting in oneself, or others or both, attract pain *karma*. – Ibid. 6.11-12
>
> The inflow of view-deluding *karma* is caused by maligning the *jinas*, their scripture, religious order and doctrine and the gods and goddesses. The inflow of conduct-deluding *karma* is caused by the highly-strung state of the soul due to the rise of the passions. – Ibid. 6.14-15

In addition to the four passions listed above, the commentaries list nine quasi passions: laughter, relish, ennui, grief, fear, abhorrence, feminine sexuality, masculine sexuality, hermaphroditic sexuality (ibid. 6.15).

The text then specifies that varying degrees of these *karmas* lead to infernal, animal and human births:

> Virulent aggression and extreme possessiveness lead to birth in the infernal realm. Deceitfulness leads to birth in animal realms.

> Attenuated aggression, attenuated possessiveness and a soft-hearted and straightforward nature, lead to birth in the human realm.
> – Ibid. 6.16-18

The text also states that self-restraint and purging of *karma* lead to birth in the realm of the gods (ibid. 6.20), though this is not the same as the ultimate goal of freedom from all *karmas*. The qualities required for this freedom are sixteenfold:

1. Purity of world view,
2. humility,
3. obeying the mores and abstinences,
4. persistent cultivation of knowledge,
5. dread of worldly existence,
6. charity,
7. austerity according to one's capacity,
8. establishing harmony and peace in the monastic order,
9. rendering service to the nuns and monks,
10. pure devotion to the adorable one,
11. pure devotion to the spiritual teacher,
12. pure devotion to the learned monks,
13. pure devotion to the scriptures,
14. regard for compulsory duties,
15. proper practice and promotion of spiritual path, and
16. adoration of the learned ascetics in the scripture.

Each of these qualities, whether of the negative type listed above or those that lead to the realm of the gods or to freedom, affirm the philosophy of voluntarism and free will that characterize Jainism.

Just as wilful *karma* delivers individual souls into repeated births in the infernal, earthly and heavenly realms, the practice of vows reverses this process. The seventh chapter of the *Tattvārthasūtra* explains the five major vows, the seven supplementary observances and the ultimate act of Jain will: the fast unto death. The five major vows are: abstinence from violence, falsehood, stealing, carnality and possessiveness (ibid. 7.1) and the seven supplementary vows to be followed by lay people are:

- refraining from movement beyond a limited area;
- restricting movement to an even more limited area;
- refraining from wanton destruction of the environment by thought, word or deed;
- keeping aloof from sinful conduct for a set period of time;
- fasting on sacred days and observing special restrictions at secluded places;
- limiting the use of consumable and non-consumable goods; and
- offering alms to wandering ascetics (ibid. 7.16).

Specific details are given for monastics and lay people for the practice of these vows, including dietary and hygiene requirements.

The commentary on the eighth chapter states that there are 180 forms of action that cause bondage and the adherence of kārmic particles that obscure the purity of the soul, prompted by greed and delusion, anger and violence. Due to one's actions, one obtains status within the realms of hell beings, subhumans, humans and gods. The text states that good *karma*s result in "pleasure, auspicious lifespan, auspicious body and auspicious status" (ibid. 8.26). The ninth chapter advocates moral behaviour as the key spiritual advancement along the fourteen stages that lead to freedom (Chapple 2003: 36). The text defines morality as "perfect forgiveness, humility, straightforwardness, purity, truthfulness, self-restraint, austerity, renunciation, detachment and continence" (*Tattvārthasūtra* 9.6). Additionally, *karma* can be sloughed off by enduring twenty-two hardships such as "hunger, thirst, cold, heat, insect bites" and so forth (ibid. 9.9).

The text also specifies six external austerities, six internal austerities and nine types of penance. Two types of meditation are prescribed for liberation, "analytic and white" (ibid. 9.30), that are said to arise among those who have perfected self-restraint and have eliminated passions. Will is required to adhere to the vows and to overcome the influence of past *karmas*. One is then able to enact the four varieties of white meditation:

i. Multiple contemplation,
ii. unitary contemplation,
iii. subtle infallible physical activity, and
iv. irreversible stillness (ibid. 9.43).

All of these efforts find their crescendo when "there is no fresh bondage because the causes of bondage have been eliminated and all destructive *karmas* have worn off" (ibid. 10.2). With this moment of freedom, the efforts of all spiritual exertion have borne fruit, delivering the soul forever more from the cycle of rebirth.

The *Tattvārthasūtra*, in philosophy, style and genre, is similar to that found in the *Yogasūtra*, the *Sāṁkhyā-kārikā* and the *Visuddhimagga*, asserts that human action determines the nature of the feeling-tone of the world that one occupies. The *karma* theory in all these texts allows no space for external agency. No creation narrative is offered. Though great figures, such as Mahāvīra, the unnamed *Īśvara* or the Buddha, may serve as exemplars and provide inspiration, they cannot intervene to create or alter *karmas*. Responsibility for one's *karma* lies solely within the creative powers of each individual.

The Yogadr̥ṣṭisamuccaya

Haribhadra Yakini Putra (*c*.700-770 CE) composed a text on comparative approaches to spiritual discipline called the *Yogadr̥ṣṭisamuccaya*. In this work, he provides a critique of various non-Jain schools, including Tantra, Advaita Vedānta, Buddhism and attachment to unclear thinking. He gently asserts that steady practice in accord with scripture is required for spiritual advancement. Following the tradition of Mahāvīra and Umāsvāti summarized above, Haribhadra proclaims the reality of the soul, the reality of *karma* and the centrality of action both in terms of worldly creation and freedom.

Referring to the rituals that require forbidden behaviour as part of a purificatory process in the Tantra, Haribhadra, in *Yogadṛṣṭisamuccaya* 72, states:

> [S]tepping into licentiousness is not stepping toward the highest goal. Indeed, the only step to be taken by *yogīs* is toward sanctioned behaviour. – Chapple 2003: 119

With great emotion, *Yogadṛṣṭisamuccaya* 84 states:

> [L]ike baited meat on a fishhook, they are addicted to vanity, decadent pleasures, and cruel behaviour. Cruel and lethargic, they renounce the true object of desire. What a pity!
> – Ibid.: 122

In regard to unclear thinking, *Yogadṛṣṭisamuccaya* 87-88 makes the following observation:

> *Fallacious argument produces in the mind*
> *sickness of intellect, destruction of equanimity,*
> *disturbance of faith and cultivation of pride.*
> *In many ways, it is the enemy of existence.*
> *The proponents of liberation*
> *are not tied to the pursuit of these fallacious arguments.*
> *However, the great souled ones are joined*
> *to scripture, good action, and samādhi.* – Ibid.: 122-23

In opposition to the teachings of Buddhism that deny abiding presence, Haribhadra claims that Buddhist doctrines comprise an incipient form of illusionism. For Jains, the reality of soul and matter cannot be denied. *Yogadṛṣṭisamuccaya* 195 states that "Something that is always being destroyed cannot be posited" (ibid.: 145). He holds a similar critique in *Yogadṛṣṭisamuccaya* 198 for the monism espoused in Advaita Vedānta: "If only a singular essence is proclaimed, then there could never be the two states of life" (ibid.: 148), implying that without the reality of happiness and misery there would be no incentive to take up spiritual purifications. *Yogadṛṣṭisamuccaya* 204-05 mentions:

If an ailment is a non-existent (as per the Vedāntins),
or is something else (as the Buddhists claim),
... then a liberated one is not liberated! – Ibid.: 147

According to Jainism, both Vedānta and Buddhism fall short of the mark because of their reluctance to take the pains of the world sufficiently seriously. *Yogadṛṣṭisamuccaya* 5 asserts the efficacy of human action in the world:

Effort (sāmarthya) Yoga is known as the highest Yoga.
It arises from an abundance of power (śakti)
stemming from the steadfast observance of the precepts.
It is the dwelling place of the accomplished ones.
– Ibid.: 104

Spiritual practice, generally referred to by the term *yoga*, requires dropping away all attachments to *karma*, a process known as disjunction (*ayoga* or *nirjarā*). This can only take place through assiduous adherence to the purifying vows. *Yogadṛṣṭisamuccaya* 11 says:

[T]he *yoga* of total freedom (*ayoga*) is declared the highest of *yogas*. Characterized by the renunciation of all things, it is truly the path of liberation. – Ibid.: 106

The religious life is summarized as the process of wilful activity in the verse 17 of *Yogadṛṣṭisamuccaya*:

Bringing about positive (sat) *activity*
by battling negative (asat) *activity*
is considered an awakened view.
From this, one is joined to true faith. – Ibid.: 107

Several activities are prescribed in *Yogadṛṣṭisamuccaya* 28 to cultivate these positive behaviours, including the advice that

> through books, worship, giving, listening and speaking, one is uplifted, as well as through teaching study, reflection, and meditation. – Chapple 2003: 109

Using the metaphor of eight different forms of fire, *Yogadṛṣṭisamuccaya* 183-84 sets forth eight different pathways[1] that lead one toward freedom from all *karma*. Through these *yogas*, one achieves "freedom from all adversity":

> *With the various species of* karma *in a purified state,*
> *the* jīva *becomes established in a cool, moonlike radiance.*
> *With respect to the world, ordinary consciousness*
> *is like a cloud concealing the moonlight.*
> *It is said that at the time*
> *when the clouds of destructive* karma
> *are themselves destroyed by the winds of* yoga,
> *that is the escape.*
> *Then the glory of singular knowledge is born.*
> – Ibid.: 142

For Haribhadra, *yoga* entails human spiritual effort. By engaging the aesthetic practices of Jain *yoga*, one is able to dispel the clouds of *karma* and rise up into a space of total freedom.

Divine Will, Human Will

The question of divine will does not arise in the Jaina tradition. In his introduction to the *Paramātmāprakāśa* of Yogindu, Upadhye states:

> ... neither *arhat* nor *siddha* has on him the responsibility of

---

[1] The eight include friendliness, protection, power, shining, firmness, pleasing, radiance and highest *yoga*, corresponding to Patañjali's eight limbs of abstinence, observance, postures, breath control, inwardness, concentration, meditation and *samādhi*. Haribhadra takes the further step of using the names of goddesses to describe these stages: Mitrā, Tārā, Bālā, Diprā, Sthirā, Kāntā, Prabhā and Parā.

> creating, supporting and destroying the world. The aspirant receives no boons, no favours and no curses from him by way of gifts from the divinity. The aspiring souls pray to him, worship him and meditate on him as an example, as a model, as an ideal that they too might reach the same condition. – Sogani 2001: 199

Those souls who have achieved liberation dwell in the highest state possible. However, they hold no power over those who remained mired in the cycle of life and death and rebirth. Their example may inspire others to hasten in their process on the path to release. As noted by Sogani:

> The ultimate responsibility of emancipating oneself from the turmoil of the world falls upon one's own undivided efforts, upon the integral consecration of energies to the attainment of divine life. Thus, every soul has the right to become *Paramātman*, who has been conceived to be the consummate realization of the divine potentialities. – Ibid.: 200

In some regards, this sets Jainism apart from other religions that originated in India. The only god to be worshipped is an indwelling god. By purifying and releasing all kārmic obstructions, human beings have the potential to connect with that point of consciousness. Though few have done so,[2] the liberated souls remain inspiring for those that strive to follow in their steps.

The Soul without Attachment, according to Kundakunda

Kundakunda, an important early Digambara writer, most likely lived in between the fifth and third century CE. His two primary texts, the *Pravacanasāra* and the *Samayasāra*, attribute qualities to the soul that underscore their independent and self-determining natures. He also clearly articulates themes well known in other traditions of India: the undying nature of the soul and the perdurability of

[2] According to the Jain tradition, the last human to achieve total liberation was the monk Jambū, who died in 463 BCE, sixty-four years after the death of Mahāvīra.

two realms of existence: the provisional and transient (*vyavahāra*), in contrast with the undying consciousness (*caitanya*), bliss (*sukha*) and energy (*vīrya*) of the liberated soul (*niścaya*).

The *Pravacanasāra* asserts that impure actions result from one's own efforts. Johnson notes that "bondage – life in *saṁsāra* – is the direct result of particular states of consciousness which are self-generated" (1995: 120). Human beings make decisions that lead to impure actions (*aśubha-karma*). In order to reverse this process, purification (*śuddha*) through adherence to vows is needed. Negative undertakings cause molecules or atoms (*skandha*) to adhere to the soul, which itself are without form or materiality. In other words, acts of will cause the soul to partake in *saṁsāra* and perpetuate its own difficulties. Similarly, acts of will are needed to reverse course and move toward freedom.

As found in other systems of Indian thought, attraction (*rāga*), repulsion (*dveṣa*) and delusion (*moha*) are at the heart of all fettering *karmas*, according to Kundakunda. This brew of *karmas* results in the emergence of a fixed sense of ego. Johnson translates verse 2.91 of the *Pravacanasāra*:

> Who does not know thus the *Paramātman*, encountered in their own natures, conceives through delusion the idea "I am (this), this is mine".
> – 1995: 139

In other words, the presence of *rāga*, *dveṣa* and *moha* results in attachment to a fixed identity which covers the true or highest self.

As with the Sāṁkhya system and the descriptions of freedom in Pāli Buddhist literature, in *Pravacanasāra* 2.98-99, Kundakunda sees the abandonment of ego as the key to freedom:

> He who does not abandon the idea of "mine" with regard to body and possessions – (thinking) "I am (this), this is mine"– gives up the state of being a *śramaṇa* and becomes one who has resorted to the wrong road. He who meditates in concentration, thinking "I am not others" and they are not mine; "I am one (with)

> knowledge", comes to be a meditator on the (pure) self.
> – Ibid.: 140

Internal purity (*śuddhopāyayoga*), enacted through adherence to non-violence, brings the aspirant away from kārmic bondage. Eventually, meditation itself becomes the vehicle for release.

In the final analysis, the second last verse of *Pravacanasāra* 3.74 proclaims that inner purity, which is also reflected in one's activities in the external world, results in faith, knowledge and freedom:

> He, who is pure, is said to be a *śramaṇa*; to the pure one belong faith and knowledge; the pure one attains liberation; he alone is a *siddha*: my salutation to him. – Ibid.: 229

Right knowledge and right action purify the soul. Kundakunda shares that equanimity (*sāmāyika*) is also needed for the realization of the highest self. In *Pravacanasāra* 2.67-68, he indicates that even being self-pleased with one's virtuous behaviour must be abandoned:

> Free from inauspicious manifestation of consciousness, not joined to auspicious (manifestation of consciousness) towards other substance, let me be indifferent (i.e. neutral); I meditate on the self whose self is knowledge. I am neither body, nor mind, nor speech, nor the cause of these, neither the agent, nor the instigator, nor the approver of doers/actors. – Johnson 1995: 203

Kundakunda's *Samayasāra* 16 elaborates on the theme of overcoming attachment within the realm of conventional reality (*saṁsāra*). The three core practices of right view, right thought and right action must be practised, though from an ultimate point of view, attachment to their "rightness" must also be renounced:

> Right belief, knowledge, and conduct should always be practised by a *sādhu* [from the *vyavahāra* point of view]; but know that these three are in, reality, the self. – Ibid.: 240

In the *Pravacanasāra*, Kundakunda explains attachment in terms of the adherence (*upayoga*) of *karmas*. In the *Samayasāra* the term *bhāva* indicates emplacement and attachment within the morass of *karmas*. As Johnson points out, "the liberated self is ... *bhāva*-less" (ibid.: 267). *Samayasāra* 183 states:

> When the *jīva* has this true knowledge, then the self, which is pure consciousness, produces no *bhāvas* whatsoever. – Ibid.: 269

Paradoxically, *Samayasāra* 127 states that the liberated one's *bhāva* has no *bhāva*:

> The *bhāva* of an ignorant person consists of ignorance; through that he produces *karmas*. But the knower's *bhāva* consists of knowledge and therefore he does not produce *karmas*.
>
> – Ibid.: 269-70

Returning to the earlier theme of freedom from possession and ego, *Samayasāra* 300 poses the following question:

> What wise man, indeed, knowing all *bhāvas* to have arisen from non-self (*parā*), and knowing that the self is pure, would utter the words, "This is mine"? – Ibid.: 270

By abandoning all claims to the self-bound by hatred (*dveṣa*), greed (*rāga*) and delusion (*moha*), one moves toward purity and freedom.

Kundakunda's assessment of will, while acknowledging its power in the creation and manipulation of the realm of phenomena (*vyavahāra*), states that will or intention even to follow the rules must eventually be discarded. The practices must become automatic, reflexive. The vows play an important role in the process of purification, but Kundakunda, in *Samayasāra* 262-65, implies that while from all outward appearances a *sādhu* will continue to live according to the vows, all pride and attachment to their perfection must disappear:

> Bondage is brought about by what is resolved (*adhyavasana*) whether one kills beings or not. ... Similarly, the resolution to lie, to take what is not given, to be unchaste, and to acquire property leads to the bondage of bad (*pāpa*) *karma*, whereas the resolution to be truthful, to take only what is given, to be chaste, and not

> to acquire possessions leads to the bondage of good (*puṇya*) *karma*. For *jīvas*, resolutions occur with reference to an object, but bondage is not caused by that object; bondage is caused by resolution [i.e. by the attitude towards the object].
>
> – Johnson 1995: 272

The power of will entangles one in *saṁsāra*; enactment of will through the performance of action in accord with the five great vows helps release one from *saṁsāra*. Kundakunda states that the true nature of the soul is that of the knower, and that "in reality it cannot and can never have been associated with the impure knowledge-restricting not self" realm of *karma* (ibid.: 282). Through action, one becomes trapped in *karma*; through action one can start to regain a sense of one's true identity as not having any claim on anything, including the notion of self. Meditation, an act of will to undo the will, provides the path to that realization.

Samaṇa Suttaṁ

In an attempt to foster inter-denominational dialogue within the Jain communities, human rights and land redistribution activist Vinoba Bhave (1895–1982), a primary successor to Mahatma Gandhi, encouraged a series of meetings to create a unified text, *Samaṇa Suttam*, acceptable to all Jain communities, to communicate their core ideas. Many of the passages emphasize the efficacy of human effort in the areas of personal improvement and social uplift. First released in 1974 and published in English translation in 1993, it conveys a sense of the antiquity and ongoing relevance of this living faith.

The text includes four parts: Source of Illumination, Path of Liberation, Metaphysics and Theory of Relativity. Its brief verses convey the broad strokes of Jainism, beginning with an invocation:

> May the path of emancipation be shown to me by the liberated souls who have freed themselves from the eight kinds of *karmas*, have attained complete fulfilment, have freed themselves from the cycles of births and deaths, and who have known the essence

> of all things. – *Samaṇa Suttam* 8

The practitioner of Jainism is hailed with martial-like imagery. The text describes the spiritual quest as a process of "gaining victory":

> He, who has gained victory over his senses and meditates on the very nature of the soul, is not bound by *karmas*; how can the *prāṇa* which is made of kārmic matter follow such a being? – Ibid. 63

> One's unconquered self, unconquered passions, and uncontrolled sense organs are one's own enemies. Oh, monk! having conquered them I move about righteously. One may conquer thousands and thousands of enemies in an invincible battle, but the supreme victory consists in conquest over one's self. – Ibid. 124-25

> After building a citadel with his right faith, gate bars with his austerities and self-control, strong ramparts with his forgiveness, invincible guards with his three controls of mind, speech and action, a monk arms himself with a bow of his penance, pierces through the garb of his *karma*, wins the battle and becomes liberated from this mundane worldly life. – Ibid. 286-87

The text also employs non-martial metaphors, likening the accomplished Jain monk to an array of animals and aspects of nature:

> Monks who are in search of the supreme path of liberation resemble a lion in fearlessness, an elephant in dignity, a bull in strength, a deer in uprightness, a beast in freedom from attachment, the wind in being companionless, the sun in brilliance, an ocean in serenity, the Mandāra mountain in firmness, the moon in coolness, a diamond in lustre, the earth in patience, a serpent in being houseless, and the sky in not being dependent. – *Samaṇa Suttam* 337

Unlike Sāṁkhya and even the *Bhagavadgītā* which claims the self is not the "doer", according to Jainism the self or soul is the doer of all actions, intentionally scripting one's self-built kārmic world:

> The soul is the doer and enjoyer of both happiness and misery; it is his own friend when it acts righteously and foe when it acts

unrighteously. – *Samaṇa Suttam* 123

The text, echoing similar statements by Socrates and the *Bhagavadgītā*, employs the metaphor of controlling the senses as one controls a horse:

> Just as a horse can be controlled by a bridle, the sensual pleasures and passions can be forcefully kept under control by knowledge, meditation, and power of penance. – Ibid. 131

The insistence on human agency finds repeated emphasis in the *Samaṇa Suttam.* The text also carefully points out that attachment to one's goodness presents an obstacle to freedom:

> He who aspires for merit, i.e. worldly well-being, aspires for life in this mundane world. Merit (*puṇya*) is capable of securing a pleasant state of existence, but it is cessation of merits only that leads to liberation. Know that an inauspicious *karma* results in misery while an auspicious *karma* results in worldly happiness. But how can it be that auspicious *karma* results in happiness when it leads to mundane existence? Just as a fetter was made of iron or gold binds a person, similarly *karma* whether auspicious (*puṇya*) or inauspicious (*pāpa*) binds the soul. Therefore, do not develop attachment for or association with either of them. – Ibid. 199-202

Equanimity, not goodness is required for liberation.

Repeatedly, the *Samaṇa Suttaṁ* advocates ethical behaviour of the highest order as the course to be followed:

> Know that Right Conduct consists in desisting from inauspicious activity and engaging in auspicious activity. The *jina* has ordained ... the observance of vows, acts of carefulness and of control. Even a person possessing scriptural knowledge will not attain emancipation if he is not able to observe strictly the activities of austerity and self-control. – Ibid. 263-64

The text gives specific ways in which the five primary vows must be practised, starting with non-violence (*ahiṁsā*):

> One should not tie, injure, mutilate, load heavy burdens, or

deprive good and drink from any animal or human due to being with a mind polluted by anger or other passions. Refraining from falsehood is the second vow. Falsehood is of five kinds: speaking untruth about unmarried girls, speaking untruth about animals, speaking untruth about lands, repudiating debts or pledges, and giving false evidence. Making a false charge, divulging anyone's secret, disclosing the secrets confided to by one's own wife, giving false advice and preparation of a false document or writing: these should be avoided. One should desist from buying stolen property, inciting another to commit theft, avoiding the rules of government, using false weights and measures, using counterfeit coins and notes. One should refrain from having intercourse with a woman kept by a vagabond or with one looked after by none, from committing unnatural sex acts, from marrying twice, and from intense desire for the sexual act. Persons should refrain from accumulation of unlimited property due to unquenchable thirst or greed as it becomes a pathway to hell. A righteous and pure-minded person should not exceed the self-imposed limit in the acquisition of lands, gold, wealth, servants, cattle, vessels and pieces of furniture. – *Samaṇa Suttam* 310-16

In addition, the daily life of the monk must include six obligatory duties:

Equanimity (*sāmāyika*), prayer to the twenty-four *jinas*, obeisance (*vandanā*), repentance (*pratikramaṇa*), bodily steadiness to meditate upon the soul (*kāyotsarga*), and renouncing future evil acts (*pratyākhyāna*). – Ibid. 422

Through all these practices, the monk achieves admirable qualities:

The (real) monks are free from attachment, self-conceit, companionship and egotism, they treat impartially and equally all living beings, whether mobile or immobile. A real monk maintains his equanimity, in success and failure, happiness and misery, life and death, censure and praise and honour and dishonour.
– Ibid. 346-47

In this way, a monk prevents the influx of *karmas* through

> inauspicious door of every kind and becomes engrossed in his rigorous self-control and discipline through spiritual meditation. – *Samaṇa Suttam* 350

Through enactment of religious vows, the monk eschews *karma* and moves toward freedom.

Despite its repeated praise of the monastic lifestyle, the text also takes a very positive view of the spiritual potential of lay life:

> While observing the vow of *sāmāyika* (refraining from sinful acts and practising mental equanimity), a householder becomes equal to a saint. – Ibid. 327

Acknowledging that a bad monk is worse than a pious layperson, the text maintains that "Apparel is no proof of a person's being self-controlled" (ibid. 356) and that "Fools put on various types of insignia [...] and maintain that this outer mark provides the path to liberation" (ibid. 358). While maintaining that renunciation of possessions is key to the spiritual life, it also points out that one must have the will power to control the mind as well:

> Renunciation of external possessions is the cause of mental purity. Renunciation of external possessions is futile if it is not combined with the internal resolve on non-attachment.
> – Ibid. 361

In summary, the Jain spiritual aspirant must engage in ethical behaviour, equanimity and meditation:

> If a person who is free from attachment, hatred, delusion and activities of the mind, speech and body, he becomes filled with the fire of meditation which burns the auspicious and inauspicious *karmas*. – Ibid. 487

By engaging the will with the intention of purification, one advances toward the goal of final release.

Field Studies of Jain Communities

Since 1990, many studies have emerged about living communities of Jains in India and abroad. Though there is not sufficient space in this chapter to provide an exhaustive account of this fieldwork, important confirmation of the Jain philosophy of free will can be gleaned from some of these resources. Two studies of Vallely and Kelting will be cited, followed with a brief account of some of my own encounters with the Jain community.

Anne Vallely lived for many months with the Terāpantha Śvetāmabara community in Ladnun, western Rajasthan. Her fascinating account includes that the religious observances of Jains include devotion, a love for the leaders of the living monastic communities as well as a sort of adoration for the twenty-four *tīrthaṅkaras*. She writes:

> Devotion (*bhakti*) permeates ascetic life. It motivates Jains of all ages to "renounce the world" and join monastic life; it motivates parents to "give their children away" [to monastic orders]; it motivates *tapas* [strict adherence to vows] and even *santhārā* [the final fast]. The discourse of devotion that underpins ascetic practices suggests a desire to belong to or connect with someone or something great than the self is central to the monastic life. Devotion makes the more austere aspects of ascetic life comprehensible and desirable by making them immediate and personal. Although the ultimate purpose of the ascetic life is to wear away *karma* and prepare the soul for emancipation, devotion makes these transcendental and abstruse goals concrete, coherent, and even joyous. – Vallely 1993: 194-95

As Vallely recounts the extreme rigours of Jain monastic life as she observed them during her residence in Ladnun from December 1995 to January 1997, she also notes the sense of religious exuberance that makes the practice of Jainism somewhat more joyful. Even somewhat routine observances such as fasts are celebrated and praised within the community, an occurrence that I also have witnessed. Rather than being a sombre, solitary undertaking, monastic life requires involvement in community, both monastic and lay. To underscore this point, Vallely quotes the founder of the Terāpantha order, Ācārya Bhikṣu (1726–1803): "Living in a group, I feel my aloneness" (ibid.: 170).

W. Kelting provides further evidence of the role of devotionalism in the boosting of religious willpower. Having resided with a lay community of Jains in Pune, India, from September 1994 to September 1995, she witnessed and narrated a profound sense of how deep emotions of love and affection motivate the practice of Jainism. Kelting begins each chapter of her book with a *stavana*, a devotional poem-song composed and shared by women in their homes and in the temple. In an idiom familiar to scholars of Mirābāī and Sūrdās and Kabīr and other countless other Indian poet-saints, these verses extol the wonders of the liberated ones and implore them to provide inspiration to proceed in the spiritual path with greater intent. One such poem-song, "Just Once, Lord Pārśva", gives a sense of the intensity of the singer's request:

Just once, Lord Pārśva, Come to my temple!
Come to my temple, that's my request.
My request is that you come, I beg you to do this.
That is my song's devoted wish.
Dark and daylight, my heart is large,
Thus, I came respectfully to you.
With the flowers of the soul, I spoke to you.

– Kelting 2001: 114

Women gather regularly to share and sing and learn such songs from one another. The *stavana* serves to reinforce Jain theology among its adherents. It performs an important social function, allowing women to gather and enjoy one another's company. It provides an outlet for creative expression and solidifies the women's importance within Jain worship. The *stavana* also allows some room for a creative interpretation of the faith, creating a context for women to respond to the paradoxical task of petitioning to, in Lawrence Babb's words, an "absent Lord" (Babb 1996). Kelting notes that in

> orthodox theological texts the *jina* is completely impervious to the demands of devotees [unlike Kṛṣṇa who assists Draupadī]. In spite of colliding headlong with the orthodox tradition, the *stavanas* abound with [...] requests [...]. For a laywoman, to ask for help in being a better Jain is not considered a worldly act but rather the opposite; it is considered a piously religious act.
>
> – Kelting 2009: 134

One form of expressing religious devotion is through the effort of singing, an important meditative undertaking in the Jain community.

In drawing this chapter to a close, I would like to share an experience of visiting the Jain Center of Southern California in Buena Park. A magnificent structure, recently rebuilt in traditional style with marble and sandstone carvings imported from India, the community areas of the complex include bas-relief sculptures that announce and celebrate the vows and some *mantras* in both English and Gujarati. The lecture hall area includes a large inscription of the *ṇamokāra mantra*, the standard prayer spoken and sung by all Jains:

> I surrender to the Ones who are enlightened and have no enemy (*arhants*; *tīrthaṅkaras*); I surrender to the Released Spirits (*siddhas*); I surrender to the wise *gurus* (*ācāryas*); I surrender to the spiritual teachers (*upādhyāyas*); I surrender to the seekers of enlightenment (*sādhus*/*sādhvīs*). – Vallely 1993: 200

By devoting oneself to these five exemplary communities, including the living heads of religious orders, teachers, monks and nuns, one manifests an intent to emulate their resolve.

Some years ago, I sat in Ladnun with Ācārya Tulsī, then head of the Terāpantha Śvetāmabara community, and asked him about the environmental ethics. He pointed to his possessions, gathered in a small bundle around him and said, this: the practice of the Jain vows holds the key to solving this problem. For Jain teachers, all joys and troubles in life are the result of human yearning. By harnessing desire, by adapting a lifestyle that orients one toward minimization of harm and possessions, personal change can be affected that will result in social uplift. Although recognizing the importance of community support and the need to find inspiration in the lives of the departed saints, Jainism remains a solitary, heroic undertaking, a commitment to purify the soul of *karma* through the constant, mindful enactment of spiritual discipline.

Acknowledgement

Portions of this paper appeared as a book chapter titled "Free Will and Voluntarism in Jainism" in *Free Will, Agency, and Selfhood in India Philosophy*, ed. Matthew R. Dasti and Edwin F. Bryant; and published by Oxford University Press, New York in 2014.

References

Babb, L., 1996, *Absent Lord: Ascetics and Kings in a Jain Ritual Culture*, Berkeley, CA: University of California Press.

Chapple, C.K. (ed.), 2003, *Reconciling Yogas: Haribhadra's Collection of Views on Yoga - with a New Translation of Haribhadra's Yogadṛṣṭisamuccaya*, tr. C.K. Chapple and J.T. Casey, Albany, NY: State University of New York Press.

"Free Will and Voluntarism in Jainism", in *Free Will, Agency, and Selfhood in Indian Philosophy*, ed. M.R. Bryant, pp. 68-84, New York: Oxford University Press, 2014.

Jaina Sūtras (*The Ācārāṅgasūtra, The Kalpasūtra*), vol. I, tr. H. Jacobi, Delhi: Low Price Publications, 1968.

Johnson, W.J., 1995, *Harmless Souls: Karmic Bondage and Religious Change in Early Jainism with Special Reference to Umāsvāti and Kundakunda*, Delhi: Motilal Banarsidass.

Kelting, W., 2001, *Singing to the Jinas: Jain Laywomen, Mandal Singing, and the Negotiations of Jain Devotion*, New York: Oxford University Press.

———, 2009, *Heroic Wives: Rituals, Stories and the Virtues of Jain Wifehood*, New York: Oxford University Press.

Monier-Williams, M., 1899, *A Sanskrit-English Dictionary*, Oxford: Clarendon Press.

Sogani, K.C., 2001, *Ethical Doctrines in Jainism*, Solapur: Jain Sanskriti Sanrakshak Sangh.

Umāsvāti/Umāsvami, 1994, *Tattvārthasūtra: That Which Is*, tr. N. Tatia, Delhi: Motilal Banarsidass.

Vallely, A., 2002, *Guardians of the Transcendent: An Ethnography of a Jain Ascetic Community*, Toronto: University of Toronto Press.

Varni, J., 1993, *Samaṇa Suttam*, ed. S. Jain, and tr. T.K. Tukol and K.K. Dixit, Varanasi: Sarva Seva Sangh Prakashan.

5

Concept of Free Will in Theravāda Buddhism

Bimalendra Kumar

THE Buddha preached the doctrine of free will or freedom. The world is impermanent, imbued with suffering and it is therefore imperative to leave it behind. The main objective of the Buddha's teachings is not to improve the world of society by introducing new ideas, norms and structures, but to cultivate moral states of mind in the human being so as to avoid conflicts. Improvement of the state of the society can take place only through the moral and spiritual improvement of each individual. After improving oneself, the individual can contribute to the society by preaching and being a good example for others to follow. Buddhism, being a psycho-ethical thought and practice, prescribes the path of freedom by not involving oneself in the internal and external problems. The Buddha's concern was neither political nor social, but purely for the freedom or liberation of the individual. The Buddha's aim followed from his concentration on the suffering at an individual level of people who were seeking freedom.

The concept of freedom has been discussed by many Western scholars. However, some scholars are of the opinion that freedom has no place in Buddhism. Walpola (1972: 54-55) observes that if existence is relative, conditioned and interdependent, how can "will" alone be free? Will, which is included in the fourth aggregate (*saṅkhārakkhandha*) of the *pañca-skandha*, like any other thought is conditioned – *paṭiccasamuppanna*. The so-called freedom itself in this world is not completely free; it, too, is conditioned and relative. The very idea of free will is not free from conditions. Jayatilleke (1972: 1-14) also examined this problem and states the reality of human freedom, without denying at the same time that it is conditioned but not wholly shaped by determinants. Freedom of choice is the very basis of Buddhist ethics. The very possibility of our refraining from evil and doing good depends on the fact that our decisions are not strictly and wholly determined and, in this sense, they are free. Thus, Buddhism upholds a theory of non-deterministic causal conditioning along with the doctrine of free will.

The Buddha advised the practitioners to cultivate the four sublime states of mind technically known as *brahmavihāra*. The follower basically tries to purify his mind from ill-will and violence, by permeating the whole world with boundless friendliness (*mettā*) and compassion (*karuṇā*), with the ambition of eventually attaining final liberation. The habitual practice of this meditation manifests in daily activities of the meditator. His actions became gradually more altruistic and this is definitely for the benefit and welfare of others. The Buddha also directed laypeople to observe the five moral precepts as an integral part of their life, to lay the basis for future spiritual development. They ensure that men and women may live peacefully, without harming the interest of others, while at the same time securing their own safety and welfare. They also enact the cultivation of the corresponding positive qualities for the society as a whole. The spiritual perfection of individuals was the single aim of the Buddha.

Buddhism accepts the doctrine of free will. The Buddhist theory of dependent origination is opposed to all deterministic theories, as well as total indeterminism, which denied causal correlations in nature altogether. Taking the middle path, steering clear of both these opposing extremes, the *paṭiccasamuppanna* maintains that human actions are conditioned but not strictly determined by the factors that affect it. Therefore, according to Buddhism, man has an element of free will which makes it possible for him to choose between alternatives (Malalasekera 1990: 274).

The Buddha says that one should reflect before doing an action, whether it is conducive to harm to oneself and others. One should carry out only those actions which neither harm oneself nor others. To cultivate *sammāvāyāma* (the right effort of the noble eightfold path),[1] one must stimulate the will. As man has the freedom to choose his actions, he is responsible for his deeds and he reaps what he sows. Therefore, the Buddha exhorts man to choose what is conducive to his own well-being and happiness, and live as an island unto oneself, he must help himself, as another cannot help him – *attadīpaviharatha attasaraṇāanaññasaraṇā* (*Dīgha Nikāya*, p. 78).

In the case of one who has no control over one's sense faculties, the individual has very little freedom. Sense faculties/*indriyāṇi* refer to the six senses operating in the day-to-day life, with reference to their respective objects. When an object comes in the range of a sense organ, there is the successive internal receiving by the former. The misdeed lies in the indulgence of the sense organ and taking delight therein. Such indulgence and delightful relishing develop attachment and give rise to suffering. Thus, putting restraints over the senses is to receive the object as receiving only and not indulging therein. The man, who has no control over his sense faculties, is much confused. The man, who has control over

1 It means the fourfold efforts. They are the efforts for not allowing the immoral states which have not come into existence; efforts for destroying the immoral states which are in existence; efforts for allowing the moral states to come into existence which have not come; and efforts for helping the faster growth of moral states, which have come into existence.

his sense faculties, is free to choose between alternatives. The *Mahataṇhāsaṅkhayasutta*[2] explains that the man who gets attracted and repelled by pleasant and unpleasant senses respectively, has a mind that is limited, which means that his freedom of action is limited. On the other hand, the man who does not get attracted by pleasurable senses and repelled by unpleasant senses has a mind that is described as unlimited.[3]

Concepts expressing freedom of choice, such as energy (*viriya*), will (*chanda*), strong will (*vimāṁsā*), effort (*vāyāma*), perseverance (*ussāha*), play a prominent role in the Buddhist scheme of liberation. *Viriya* is the energy of the psychic supporting force. As a falling thatch is supported by pillars, similarly the falling mind is supported by *viriya*. *Chanda* is a strong desire to do something. *Vimāṁsā* is the name of the strong will to penetrate into the nature of something to know the truth. Man is advised to assert his freedom by overpowering evil states of the mind, just as the strong man would overpower a weak man.

When one controls one's physical sense faculties, one develops spiritual faculties such as *saddhindriya*, *viriyindriya*, *satindriya*, *samādhindriya* and *paññindriya*.[4] *Saddhā* is termed as faith, confidence or respect. It helps in removing the pollution of mind just like a water-purifying gem and makes water pure. *Viriya* is the energy of the psychic supporting force. It grants mental support and makes one firm and undisturbed in the virtuous pursuits. *Sati* means mindfulness. It is another name of mental awareness and functions

---

[2] *so cakkhunārūpaṁdisvāpiyarūperūpesārajjati, appiyarūperūpebyāpajjati, anupaṭṭhitakāyasaticaviharatiparicetaso* । *tañcacetovimuttiṁpaññāvimuttiṁyathābhūtaṁnāppajnāti* । – *Majjhima Nikāya*, vol. V, p. 338

[3] *so cakkhunārūpaṁdisvā ... upaṭṭhitakāyasati ca viharatiappamānacetaso. tañcacetvimuttiṁpaññāviṁuttiṁyathābhutaṁpajānati* । – Ibid., p. 341

[4] *bhikkhu saddhindriyaṁ bhāvetiupasamagāmiṁsambodhagāmiṁ, viriyindriyaṁbhāveti ... paññindriyaṁbhāvetiupasamagāmiṁsambodhagmiṁ* । – Ibid., p. 214

as a guard as well as a reminding force. *Samādhi* removes the mental misdeeds and prepares a congenial atmosphere for emergence of the pure consciousness. *Paññā* destroys the darkness of ignorance, penetrates into the nature of reality, makes it understandable as impermanent, subject to suffering and substanceless; it helps in uprooting the thickets of attachment and in realizing the supramundane blissful state.

There is a practice of fivefold controlling factors (*pañcindriya-bhāvanā*), viz. *saddhindriya, viriyindriya, satindriya, samādhindriya* and *paññindriya.* These five factors appear in the list of *bodhipakkhiyadhammā* twice, once as controlling factors (*indriyas*) and another time as powers (*bala*). They function in controlling the mind and directing it to the right direction in making a smooth wayfaring, beginning from the moment of practice till realization of *nibbāna.* When the spiritual faculties get further strengthened, they become powers (*bala*) such as *saddhābala* and *viriyabala.* They also function as power in exercising predominant influence on the mind in a particular state. Some of these powers are then developed to become factors of enlightenment (*bojjhaṅga*) which bring about the total unshakable liberation of the mind – *akuppācetovimutti* (cf. *Majjhima Nikāya*, vol. V, p. 214). Thus, it is possible to maintain that, by exploiting the element of free will with which man is endowed, the individual can work himself upward to completely decondition himself from the factors that affect him and thus disjoin the chain of causation. He has come to a state of unconditioned freedom from bondage and that state is generally called *nibbāna.*

The *Kālāmasutta* is the best expression of freedom of thought in Buddhism. There, the Buddha admonished the *kālāma* not to accept a proposition as true on criteria like revelation and tradition. One should accept a proposition only on grounds of personal conviction and when the resultant consequences of such acceptance are seen to be useful in the light of experience (*Aṅguttara Nikāya*, pp. 216-22). The individual is also advised to be guided by the attitude of the wise. The Buddha expects his teachings to be subjected to the same investigation as those prescribed to the *kālāma*'s and he describes his doctrines as inviting investigation and verification – *ehipassika.*[5] Furthermore, there are some mental hindrances, called *nīvaraṇas*, which retard the freedom of thought – *cetaso-upakkilesepaññāyadubbalikaraṇe* (*Majjhima Nikāya*, vol. I, p. 242). They are *kāmacchanda* (desire for sensual pleasure), *byāpāda* (hatred or antipathy), *thīnamiddha* (conscious idleness is *thīna* and psychic idleness is *middha*), *uddhaccakukucca* (brooding over of the mind) and *vicikicchā* (doubt related with the Buddha, Dhamma and Saṅgha). For real freedom, one must rid their mind of these psychological hindrances. In fact, the very aim of course of mental training in Buddhism is to create suitable conditions to allow the free arising of wisdom and that state is called *paññāvimutti* (freedom through wisdom).

Freedom of thought becomes quite meaningless, if freedom to choose between two alternative courses of action is denied. The Buddhist condemnation of dogmatism provides substantial proof to establish the point that Buddhism accepts free will. Dogmatism prevails only where there are constraints on free will and prohibition on investigation. Buddhism freely encourages investigation and inquiry (cf. "Caṅkīsutta" in *Majjhima Nikāya*, vol. II, pp. 383-92).

Buddhism also encourages the free expression of ideas. The Vajjians about whom the Buddha speaks in praise in the *Mahāparinibbāna Sutta* (*Dīgha Nikāya*, pp. 57-64) are said to assemble in unity periodically, evidently for discussing freely the affairs of the state and community problems. The Buddha says that they will continue to prosper so long as this institution of free discussion continues to function. It is recorded in the *Cullavagga*, that the Buddha has been against the idea of rendering the *Buddhavacana*

---

5 *svākkhātobhagavatādhammosandiṭṭhikoakālikoehipassikoopāneyyikopacca-ttaṁ veditabboviññuhi* । – *Aṅguttara Nikāya*, p. 237

into Chāndasa language and allowed the transmission of his words in all languages and dialects,[6] because he believed that the mother tongue allows anybody to understand and express ideas better and more freely. Here, the term *sakāyaniruttiyā* means "in its own language". In disciplinary and ecclesiastical matters, the Buddhist code of discipline requires that the Saṅgha – assembly of people who come together after removing all the discriminating factors – should be duly informed of the matters which need attention and all members are expected to express their views on the issues concerned (*Cullavagga*, p. 182). This is a clear example of the freedom of expression that is guaranteed to all members in the community of monks.

Freedom has been considered as a moral and social concept. Many *suttas* contain discussions pertaining to the question of moral freedom, and in these *suttas* one finds not only the Buddha's point of view, but also the view held by his contemporaries on this issue. As the Buddha's teaching on ethics is fundamentally related to his teachings on causality, to get a clear idea of the Buddhist position on free will, one has to study it in relation to causality. It is because such an ability is accepted that Buddhism admonishes all to accomplish what is morally good and refrain from what is morally bad – *sabbapāpassa akaraṇaṁ, kusalassaupasampadā* (*Dhammapada* 5).

In this context, the word used to denote "will" is *cetanā*, means thinking in relation to action. Being, the determinant of the psychic aspect of the individual, it plays a very important role in the operation of moral action, *kamma*. Psychologically, *cetanā* determines the activities of mental states associated with it, and ethically, it determines its inevitable consequences. The will, however, like everything else is conditioned. *Rāga* (attachment), *dveṣa* (hatred) and *moha* (ignorance) are the factors which influence the will when it makes any choice. *Cetanā* is not coerced by any

[6] *anujānāmi, bhikkhave, sakāyaniruttiyābuddhavacanaṃpariyā-punituṁti.*
– *Cullavagga*, p. 260

external factor. It is only for this type of action that one becomes morally responsible. No moral responsibility is attached to an individual who does an act without a conscious, deliberate will or who does an act with a coerced will, over which coercion the individual has no control. This is why *cetanā* is equated with *kamma*.

Thus, on the basis of the facts stated above, one comes to the conclusion that freedom is a relative concept, especially in the Buddhist context; it has a specific use as a moral and social concept. The will or freedom plays an important role in an individual's current life as well as in his/her life hereafter.

References

Aṅguttara Nikāya, vol. 1, 1998, Igatpuri: Vipassana Research Institute.

Cullavagga, 1998, Igatpuri: Vipassana Research Institute.

Dīgha Nikāya, vol. II, 1993, Igatpuri: Vipassana Research Institute.

Gupta, C. (ed.), 1968, *Dhammapada*, Varanasi: Chaukhambha Vidyabhavan.

Jayatilleke, K.N., 1972, *Ethics in Buddhist Perspective*, Kandy, Sri Lanka: Buddhist Publication Society.

Majjhima Nikāya, vols I, II & V, 1955, Igatpuri: Vipassana Research Institute.

Malalasekera, G. (ed.), 1990, *Encyclopedia of Buddhism*, Ceylon: Buddhist Council of Ceylon, Ministry of Cultural Affairs, Government of Sri Lanka.

Walpola, R., 1972, *What the Buddha Taught*, London: Gordon Fraser.

6

"Śramaṇa Ethics" Determinism in the Contemporary Context

Meenal Katarnikar

ANY discussion on the relevance of Śramaṇa ethics presupposes clarity on the term itself, otherwise it may be interpreted to be about the ethical principles meant for ascetics. This, in turn, may raise the doubt if these are the principles for monks, then what purpose do they serve for worldly people? Hence, clarification of Śramaṇa ethics is required for both the proper understanding and assertion of the term.

Śramaṇa ethics suggests the ethical value system endorsed by the philosophical schools belonging to the Śramaṇa tradition, that is to say, Jainism and Buddhism. Both these faiths have prescribed the paths for spiritual salvation, good living, quality of life and elevation of the human mind, which are relevant for both, ascetics and householders. The values and principles that occupy those paths are collectively known as Śramaṇa ethics.

Thus, Śramaṇa ethics centres around the idea of moral righteousness, according to a particular Śramaṇa tradition. It forms a well-knit structure of prominent and peripheral values that is competent to address core ethical issues. One such core issue is the problem of determinism and free will. This paper will begin with the examination of determinism in Śramaṇa ethics, then will proceed to explore their essential principles and will end with a discussion regarding the contemporary relevance of Śramaṇa ethics.

Is Śramaṇa Tradition Deterministic?

Determinism, in a broad and crude sense of the term, is a doctrine which believes that all events, including human action, are ultimately determined by causes that are regarded as external to the will. Some philosophers have taken determinism to imply that individual human beings have no free will and cannot be held morally responsible for their actions. There are many definitions of determinism, depending upon what pre-conditions are considered to be determinative of an event or action, such as theological determinism and environmental determinism.

Here, the discussion will examine whether the ethics advocated in the Śramaṇa traditions is deterministic or not, while making a passing reference to the general characteristics of determinism.

One prominent and compelling reason to refer to Śramaṇa ethics as deterministic is the world view and the associated doctrine of *karma*, which is accepted in both Jain and Buddhist systems. The Śramaṇa tradition looks at two main aspects:

i. the relation between man and the world, and
ii. the ultimate goal of human life.

It begins by self-reflecting:

> Who am I? I am a soul that is eternal, but I have a body that results from my past sinful activity. I am thrown into this world because of my *karmas* – this is not my place – and I must get rid of them to leave my physical body. To be free from the bondage of my body, I must completely renounce the world and my family ties.

That is why this tradition is called ascetic – Śramaṇa – tradition. As *mokṣa* is the highest goal, asceticism is the ideal path of life.

As the householder is on the periphery of this society, he is treated as inferior to *Śramaṇa*. This is based on the basic tenets of Jainism and only partially applicable to Buddhism. Buddhism does not accept the ultimate reality of the soul and, hence, soul-centric analysis mentioned above is not relevant to it. However, it offers a very convincing exploration of bondage in terms of suffering, which in turn is caused by ignorance and craving; and like Jainism, Buddhism too offers the eightfold noble path towards freedom from suffering. Thus, it can be said that according to the Śramaṇa tradition, the relation of man and the world is contingent on man's final goal, i.e. liberation from this world.

The cycle of birth and death, the course of life and the overall working of the universe depend upon the law of *karma*, there is no divine interference in it. However, on the basis of a sort of *karma*-determinism, it would be totally inappropriate to conclude that the Śramaṇa systems are pessimistic, or that they picture the human person as a helpless pawn in the hands of destiny. Both systems are convinced about the potential capacity of a human to break the cycle of births and deaths, and achieve final liberation. The idea of *mokṣa* in Jainism and *nirvāṇa* in Buddhism represent the state of freedom that is to be achieved by following the path in this life only.

In this line of thought, the term "determinism in the Śramaṇa tradition" makes sense only with a certain qualification as it does not represent any absolutistic doctrine. Both the traditions advocate that this *karma* determinism can be put to an end by achieving perfect knowledge and practising perfect conduct. There is neither absolutistic determinism nor absolutistic freedom according to the Śramaṇa systems. The ideas of *ghātī-aghātī karma*s, five *samavāyas* and the middle path point to the fact that human life cannot be only fatalistic, nor can it be explained away by the notion of exclusive freedom. There is freedom because there is determinism and there is conditioning because there is a ray of hope in the form of breaking that conditioning. So, determinism and freedom are not contradictory terms according to the Śramaṇa tradition, rather they are supplementary or reciprocal terms, where each acquires meaning and significance only in the context of the other.

With this deliberation, it would be helpful to have some account of the principles and concepts which work as foundational ground for the ethical theories in the two Śramaṇa traditions. These are *ahiṁsā* and Anekāntavāda in Jain tradition, and *karuṇā* and *madhyamā pratipada* in Buddhist tradition.

The Jain Principles

AHIṀSĀ

The Jains regard *ahiṁsā* (non-violence) as the virtue of all virtues, the supreme *dharma.* A lot has been said and written about this doctrine, by Jains and non-Jains, and that it has probably been interpreted quite differently from canonical and post-canonical Jain philosophical thought. However, for the proper and authentic understanding of the Jain concept of *ahiṁsā*, it is necessary to seek help from ancient canonical and philosophical texts of the Jain tradition.

Two comprehensive definitions of *ahiṁsā* are found in two texts; one is found in the *Ācārāṅgasūtra*, one of the most ancient scriptures of Jainism and the other is given in the *Tattvārthasūtra*, the first philosophical text of Jainism.

In *Ācārāṅgasūtra* 4.1.1,[1] it is said:

> [T]he *arhats* (venerable ones) of the past, those of the present and future narrate thus, discourse thus, proclaim thus, and assert thus: One should not injure, subjugate, enslave, torture or kill any animal, living being, organism and sentient being.

Umāsvāti says, "[t]he destruction of life due to an act involving

[1] *je ya atītā, je ya paduppaṇṇā, je ya agamissā aarhantā bhagavantā, te savve evamāikkhanti, evaṁ bhāsanti, evaṁ paṇṇaventi, evaṁ parūventi-savve pāṇā savve bhūtā savve jīvā save sattā ṇa hantavvā, ṇa ajjāvetavvā, ṇa parighettavvā, ṇa paritāveyavvā, ṇa uddaveyavvā* ।

negligence is violence".[2] Refraining from this defilement is non-violence.

The characteristic of non-violence is the supplement of the psycho-analysis provided therein. Mere deprivation of life or a mere causing of pain must not necessarily be treated as a cause of defilement-designated violence: besides that act what has further to be investigated is as to what was the mental feeling of the agent that actuated the act. The mental feeling is made up of various impulses of attachment and aversion, as well as negligence – a totality for which the technical designation is *pramāda*. When deprivation of life results from an evil mental feeling, it alone is a case of violence. Thus, refraining from such evil mental feelings that activates deprivation of life or causing pain will be designated as non-violence. In order to maintain a non-violent behaviour, *Tattvārthasūtra* 7.3 suggests certain activities such as being attentive to movement, keeping one's mind under guard and inspecting things that are eaten and drunk.

In the most of the religious traditions, violence is usually associated with causing harm to other living beings. Jainism primarily takes it to injuring oneself, a behaviour which inhibits the soul's ability to attain *mokṣa*. The focus on one's own spiritual progress is an important motivating factor for observing *ahiṁsā*.

Fundamental to the Jain principle of *ahiṁsā* is the belief that each living being or element (humans, animals, plants, earth, water, fire and air) possesses an individual soul. This soul is characterized by consciousness, undergoes continuous changes between various grades of purity and impurity, ignorance and knowledge. Jains hold that the soul takes up a new body after the death of its present body according to its volitional activities; *karma* particles are attracted to the soul and create a bondage that determines the lifespan, and other salient characteristics of the new body for the soul. Depending upon the volitional force, if the soul becomes subject to attachment

[2] *pramattayogāt prāṇavyaparopaṇaṁ hiṁsā* । – *Tattvārthasūtra* 7.8

and aversion, it gets tainted by *ahiṁsā* and thus becomes harmful to itself and others. If it maintains detachment and compassion, it is characterized by *ahiṁsā*.

Thus, the starting point of the Jain discussion on *ahiṁsā* is the perspective of one's own soul and not so much the standpoint of the protection of the other beings or the welfare of humanity as a whole.

The awareness of *ahiṁsā*, according to the Jains, is a constant concern for the individual, involving total mindfulness in mental, oral and physical activities – *mānasika*, *vācika* and *kāyika yoga*. In the same fashion, prohibition and refraining from violence is not limited to one's own actions, but it covers the appreciation and instigation of others' violent activities.

ANEKĀNTAVĀDA

Anekāntavāda is a central thought of Jainism. It can be translated as a theory of non-radicalism, non-absolutism, non-one-sidedness, manifoldness. A detailed study reveals that it is a philosophy of synthesis – conciling approach towards various ontological theories of ancient India.

It is well known that the doctrine of *ahiṁsā* holds supreme importance in the Jain tradition. Mahāvīra expanded this doctrine of non-violence from the sphere of practical behaviour to the sphere of intellectual, epistemological and philosophical discussion. Thus, the principle of respect for other views emerges from the principle of respect for other life. It is a doctrine that is characterized by toleration, understanding and respect for the views of the others. It is a unique character of the Jain philosophy and religion.

Anekāntavāda, with the support of its corollaries, viz. Syādvāda (conditioned viewpoints) and Naẏavāda (partial viewpoints) establishes the principle of epistemological respect of the views of others. It is mentioned by the scholars as a principle of toleration, but that is an incomplete and unjust description of the theory. For, toleration involves bearing something against ones wish as an involuntary coexistence, or any other negative feeling of the same sort. However, according to Jainism, such tolerance would be a violence done to oneself, but Anekāntavāda does not involve, expect or prescribe such non-violence to anyone. Rather, it has the great potential to eliminate violent argument between ideological opponents by methodically both disarming and persuading them, because it is a principle of respectful recognition of the other views. It fosters a sense of non-violence by reconciling opposites and making it viable for people holding opposing views to enter into dialogue and negotiate their differences, by violent confrontation.

In fact, this theory has brought to the forefront a very important truth about metaphysical theories, namely, that they are expressions of personal intellectual convictions rather than objective facts. If this is the status of metaphysical theories, then no metaphysical theory can be rejected on the ground of non-conformity to reality. Anekāntavāda emphasizes this element and hence has the potential to create the atmosphere of harmony in fields like philosophy and religion.

The basic assumption of Jainism is that each object is supposed to have innumerable aspects and hence it is possible to apply innumerable predicates to it. Yet, it then defeats the purpose of predication, as the description is supposed to distinguish one theory from the other. However, Jains attach more importance to stating the truth rather than describing a thing with definitive predication. They contend that no philosophical proposition can be true if it is only unconditionally asserted. Even the conflicting propositions of rival schools may be in order, provided they are asserted with proper conditionalization. In this sense, Anekāntavāda goes beyond pluralism and relativism. It does not merely give "permission" to diversity; it ideally mandates an encounter with it. It is only through exposure to other ways of being that the fuller picture of reality will emerge. Anekāntavāda obligates its adherents to become familiar with other ways of knowing. It can help redress the epistemological muddle in which the posts-modernists find themselves.

The Buddhist Principles

KARUṆĀ

Karuṇā denotes compassion that is empathy, rather than sympathy. The spirit of compassion flows as the undercurrent of the Buddhist thought. The tradition emerges from the Buddha's compassion towards all the beings who are wandering in the ocean of suffering. He wanted to show the path that leads to the total annihilation of suffering. This is the act of greatest compassion. And hence, the concept of compassion acquires a very significant role in Buddhist philosophy, ethics as well as spirituality.

Apart from its all-pervading influence in Buddhist tradition, *karuṇā* is prominently mentioned as the second step of the eightfold path, viz. right resolve – *samyak saṅkalpa*. Right resolve means pure mind which is free from desire, ill-will, hatred and cruelty. Instead, it is endowed with harmlessness, compassion, benevolence and loving kindness. This compassion is a quality of a pure mind which is set for *nibbāna*, the final goal. The mind which is set on enlightenment is known as *bodhicitta*. It has two aspects – the determination to attain Buddhahood and the aspiration to save the sentient beings from suffering. It is the second aspect that entails compassion, that makes the existence of the person with pure mind in this world meaningful, the refuge of all those who are afflicted.

Along with being the main characteristic of a pure mind, *karuṇā* forms the main quality or rather nature of the enlightened being – *bodhisattva*. The enlightened person attains freedom, but does not enjoy the bliss or satisfaction all alone; the person aspires for the enlightenment of others too. According to Mahāyāna Buddhism, the liberation of all sentient beings is the ultimate goal of a spiritual aspirant; a *bodhisattva* does not even mind to undergo the cycle of birth and death in order to liberate the other living beings from misery. Thus, it is no longer an ordinary compassion, but a great compassion.

> Thus, the essential nature of all *bodhisattvas* is a great essential

> heart, *mahā-karuṇā citta*, and all sentient beings constitute the objects of his love. They look on all living beings as though victims going to the slaughter. With their heart full of compassion, they work for the welfare and happiness of all beings. They seek no delight in pursuing their own salvation while their brothers and sisters are steeped in misery. Instead, they prefer to be the saviour. – Suzuki 2002: 121-22

Thus, the altruistic dimension of *karuṇā* is the foundation of the Buddhist thought.

MADHYAMĀ PRATIPADA

Madhyamā pratipada is the middle path that has conceptual affinity with Anekāntavāda, as both spring from a pre-Śramaṇic technique called Vibhajjavāda. However, Anekāntavāda resolves the issues by synthesizing the differences, whereas the middle path resolves the issues by avoiding the extremes.

After attaining the enlightenment, the Buddha was determined on his path that was independent, avoiding the two extremes of self-indulgence and self-mortification. This path is known as *madhyamā pratipada*. This path gives vision, knowledge and it leads to calm, to insight, to enlightenment and to *nibbāna*. The middle path rejects both affirmation and negation, and advocates *śūnyatā*.

According to this path, either exclusive affirmation or exclusive negation represents dogmatism which is the main cause of almost all disputes. The solution lies in realizing the futility of the extremes and moving towards the synthesis of the two; that is the real import of middle path.

Contemporary Relevance of Śramaṇa Ethics

Both the Buddhist and Jain traditions advocate values, such as non-violence, non-possessiveness, compassion, discipline and detachment, which inspire the individual to march towards the highest goal of human life, spiritual salvation. If salvation is the good, it leads to the fact that these are the values relevant for ascetics; hence, the relevance thereof for householders is in question. However, both the traditions have explored the above-mentioned values in such a manner that they can be practised by and can keep guiding the householders as the moral principles constituting the way of life. The challenge today is to examine whether these principles are capable of guiding the people in a contemporary technocrat society.

Walpola (2006: xiii) says:

> In reality, however, just as in the present even in the past, there had been only a mixture of good and bad and never there had been a perfectly blissful society.

This statement applies to any human society in the past, present and future including the contemporary society. Consequently, the aim of all human endeavours is to create peaceful, harmonious atmosphere and a perfect society where there is happiness, abundance and justice. Reality about social phenomenon is that it is a mixture of joy and sorrow, haves and have-nots, and justice and injustice.

In the contemporary context, this picture of the society is coloured by scientific and technological glitter. Science and technology have brought radical change in human life, not only in the material or consumerist context, but very effectively in human relations, value-paradigms and even human–world–Divinity relations.

It is needless to say that human society is experiencing comforts, smoothness, advanced techniques and a sort of victory-over-nature due to magnificent progress in science and technology. The explosion of information has brought about considerable changes in the sphere of knowledge; the world is now a click's distance away and within a fraction of a moment, any information is available. Accessibility of people is improved because of the virtual dimension of technology. Internet, social networking sites and mobile phones have captured and shown their strength in increasing the frequency of human relations. Food, agriculture, medicine, industry, media – no sphere of human life has remained untouched by science and technology.

Along with this bright side of science and technology, one however must be cautious of the dark side of the same. Pollution, increasing diseases, stress, anxiety, alienation in relations, minimization or even annihilation of all tenderness of emotions; these are some commonly and overtly observed effects of a technologically dominated society. But the fundamental loss is in the realm of value paradigms and ethical norms adopted by the new society; this has taken place at both individual and social levels. Deterioration of political standards, devaluation of social morality and weakening of the psychological strengths have a strong and influential undercurrent of the moral bankruptcy at both individual and social planes of human society.

Here, Śramaṇa ethics and the values endorsed by the same can supply the guidelines and help elevate the profoundness of human existence. The Śramaṇa traditions in India, viz. Jainism and Buddhism, are known for their high moral ideals such as non-violence, truth, non-possessiveness and emphasis on spiritual values such as liberation, peace, disciplined life encompassed by practising vows, an austere way of living and pursuit of *summum bonum*, the highest aim of human life. Both of them guided humanity for years together and were successful in maintaining the rule of righteousness. With this legacy and the richness of their principles, they can provide some solution to contemporary value crisis.

However, the questions in the twenty-first century are: Are these moral values and principles relevant in contemporary social and cultural conditions? Are they compatible with the age of science and technology? If they are accepted and placed before the present generation in a traditional way (with their metaphysical or dogmatic baggage), these values will not serve their purpose.

Thus, there will be a couple of challenges before this ethical paradigm. First of all, the twenty-first century society is a society that values consumption, enjoyment, power, and the life of riches, luxury and comfort. All the scientific discoveries, technological inventions and devices based on them are meant for making human life smoother in material and empirical senses. At the same time, they have made human life more dependent on as well as related to external factors. It will be a challenge to show the use and instill reverence of values like simplicity, detachment, non-violence, compassion or independence in the contemporary way of living.

Young generation adopts the scientific approach and hence, accepts only those things that are proved by evidence and rational thinking. It is a challenge to prove the propriety, acceptability and even worth of all these moral values. As the values are inclined towards spirituality which is trans-rational, it is a challenge to create empirical evidence and rational thinking to support them.

The values discussed above are of such a type that they can be justified rationally, or more categorically, without assuming any metaphysical theories or paradigms. In other words, any human person, who is leading a social life, will have to practise non-violence, middle path and compassion, irrespective of class, caste, creed or gender, if one expects harmonious and peaceful co-existence in the contemporary cosmopolitan society. Not only this, consumerism and materialism in the twenty-first century can be counterbalanced by only rationalizing simplicity and detachment. The influential technological progress is no doubt a product of human rationality, but it can dominate the psychological dimension of human personality. When the ethical concerns are in question, the same technological progress remains silent as it is ethics-neutral. Technology in itself cannot address any ethical dilemma as it belongs to a totally different dimension. It can be labelled to be ethical or unethical only by its use, through the person making its use for ethical or unethical purposes. Such a person can be provided with ethical guidance, not by technology but by philosophy. If the young generation sees this truth, it is not difficult to justify the relevance of Śramaṇa ethics in the contemporary technocrat society.

However, there is a serious structural problem regarding Śramaṇa ethics and that is its own inherent complexity. Values put forward by Śramaṇa ethics direct one to self-realization and, hence, technically it can rightly be called as individualistic ethics; their main aim is not to create a good society, rather they aim at detaching the person from social ties. Ethics necessarily has a social dimension; however what type of social dimension can be tied to these individualistic values?

Here, it can be argued that if the values discussed above are considered as independent values, as a necessary precondition of any social life, rather than as constituent of *mokṣa*-oriented Śramaṇa ethics, those individualistic values will at once acquire the social dimension required for any ethical concept. In other words, those values are considered as essential prerequisites of inter-personal relations which form the fabric of social life, rather than instrumental for some transcendent spiritual goal.

It is a call of the age to scholars and experts in the field to accept these challenges and offer an interpretation and justification of this value-paradigm so that humanity will walk in the direction of a perfectly blissful society.

References

Madhukar Muni (ed.), 1989, *Ācārāṅgasūtra*, vol. I, Beawar: Shri Agam Prakashan Samiti.

Suzuki, D., 2002, "Outlines of Mahayana Buddhism", in *Buddhanusmrti* (*A Glossary of Buddhist Terms*), ed. A. Kala, pp. 120-21, Mumbai: Somaiya Publications.

Umāsvāti, 2009, *Tattvārthasūtra*, ed. S. Sanghvi, Varanasi: Parshvanath Vidyapeeth.

Walpola, R., 2006, "Preface", in *What the Buddha Taught*, Sri Lanka: Buddhist Cultural Centre.

7

Free Will in the Realm of Morality
A Jain Perspective

Kamini Gogri

Jain ethical theory is a part of Jain soteriology. It has necessarily a reference to the Jain theory of bondage and liberation, because ethical conduct in some form is a necessary condition of liberation and unethical behaviour necessarily leads to bondage, according to Jain philosophy. How ethical conduct is understood in Jain philosophical literature and in what way it is related to bondage and liberation are the questions worth pursuing.

In this paper, the Jain theory of bondage and liberation will be first dealt with in brief. This will be done in terms of the seven basic concepts (*tattvas*) and the three jewels (*tri-ratna*). The Jain ethical approach then will be introduced in the context of their theory of bondage and liberation. As the Jain ethical theory, which is primarily the theory of right conduct, centres around the concept of *ahiṁsā*, the highest value for the Jains, the discussion on the theory of right conduct in this paper will centre on *ahiṁsā*. This doctrine gives rise to many issues of philosophical significance. Some of such issues will be raised and discussed in the second part of this paper.

The Jain Theory of Right Conduct

THE SEVEN BASIC CONCEPTS

The Jain theory of bondage and liberation can be formulated in terms of seven basic concepts (*tattvas*) and three jewels (*tri-ratna*). The seven basic concepts in classical Jainism are: *jīva* (soul), *ajīva* (non-soul), *āsrava* (inflow of *karma*-particles into the soul), *bandha* (bondage), *saṁvara* (stoppage of kārmic inflow), *nirjarā* (shedding of *karma* particles from the soul) and *mokṣa* (liberation). Unlike in Buddhism, where *duḥkha* (suffering) is the main problem of life, the main problem of life according to Jainism is *bandha* – the sticking and binding of *karma* particles to the soul. When one performs any voluntary action out of passions, such as greed, pride, anger or delusion, the soul invites *karma-pudgalas*. Jains make a subtle distinction between *karma-pudgala* and the *pudgalas* which are capable of becoming *karma*. There are certain types of material particles, which are spread over the universe, that take the form of *karmas* when a soul, due to its passions, attracts them and makes them enter into it. Those subtle material particles are then called *karma-pudgala*.[1]

Jains believe that the process of bondage has been taking place since forever but that it can come to an end. To end bondage, one has to control one's own mind, speech and behaviour in such a way that the inflow of *karma* particles stops and *karma* particles which have already stuck to the soul are gradually removed through penance; ultimately the soul will be completely purified. When the soul is completely free from *karma* particles, it is liberated.

THE NATURE OF JĪVA AND KĀRMIC BONDAGE

Jains accept *mokṣa* – absolute emancipation from kārmic bondage – as the highest goal that any living being should aim at. The final emancipation is the disembodied state of *jīva* (soul) where the *jīva* is free from any kind of body, even the subtlest kind of body, like

---

[1] *karmaṇo yogyān pudgalānādatte* – *Tattvārthasūtra* 8.2

the *kārmaṇa śarīra*. This state, when achieved, remains permanent. Naturally *jīva* is accepted as a permanent substance by Jains. But unlike other soul-affirming systems, Jainism regards this soul as a candidate for change which is called *pariṇāma* (transformation). Accordingly, *jīva* is not absolutely eternal (*kūṭastha nitya*, like *puruṣa* of Sāṁkhya or *Brahman* of Vedānta), but changing-yet-eternal (*pariṇāmī nitya*, like *prakṛti* of Sāṁkhya). In fact, this particular feature of eternality qualified by change is shared by all the substances, as accepted in Jain ontological framework. Every substance according to them has some essential features (*guṇas*, *sahabhāvī dharmas*) on account of which it remains constant, and it also has some accidental features (*paryāyas*, *kramabhāvī dharmas*) on account of which it changes. Consciousness, for instance, is the essential feature of *jīva*, whereas its association with a particular body is its accidental feature. *Jīva*, due to its association with kārmic matter, has sense organs, a mind and a physical body, and it performs various actions and it also experiences pleasures and pains. This has an implication to the Jain theory of morals, which requires the notion of a moral agent.

A moral agent should be such that he (or she or it) should be capable to perform voluntary actions and to be held responsible for the moral worth of these actions. He should be capable of enjoying fruits of those actions. He should be the agent (*kartā*) as well as the enjoyer (*bhoktā*). In Jain metaphysics, *jīva* fulfils this condition. Hence, *jīva* can be regarded as a moral agent in the Jain framework. This conception of *jīva* also supports the Jain advocacy of the doctrine of *karma*, which implies that one who performs any action must experience the fruit of it. Conversely, the one who experiences pleasure or pain must be experiencing it as a result of one's own past action. Naturally, the doctrine requires the identity of the agent and the enjoyer. According to Jain metaphysics, *jīva* possesses both the features and, hence, it becomes the proper candidate for the operation of the *karma* doctrine.

The *karma* doctrine makes another theoretical requirement that there should be a causal connection between the performance of action and the experience of fruit, although it is maintained that the fruit of an action may not be experienced immediately but after a long time-gap. In Jainism, this function is performed by the subtle physical particles of *karma* matter which stick to *jīva* when it performs physical, vocal or mental actions under the spell of passions (*Tattvārthasūtra* 6.1-5). When this *karma* matter becomes ripe for fruition (*vipāka*), it causes the experience of pleasure or pain and gets dissociated from *jīva* (*nirjarā*). This dissociation of *karma* matter from *jīva* is called *vipāka-nirjarā* (purgation by fruition). Jains believe that an ascetic can dissociate *karma* matter from *jīva* with the help of austerities, even without them coming to fruition. This latter kind of dissociation is called *avipāka-nirjarā* (purgation without fruition) (*Sarvārthasiddhi* 8.23).

It should be noted here that the term *karma* has been used in Jain literature in two senses. The first one is an ordinary sense in which *karma* means an action performed by a living being. Umāsvāti, for instance, defines *yoga* (which is a technical term in Jainism) as the action (*karma*) performed through body, speech or mind.[2] The other sense of the term is the metaphysical sense according to which *karma* means a very subtle kind of matter (*pudgala*) which is associated with the soul as soon as any action is performed. Hence, when we talk about kārmic bondage in the Jain context, we have to acknowledge both the aspects of it. It is the bondage caused by the performance of *karmas* (actions) and it is the bondage which is physically constituted by *karmas* (subtle material particles).

Jains also hold that *jīva* has always had this kārmic bondage. That is because any situation, pleasant or painful, in which *jīva* finds itself is due to the prior action performed by the same *jīva*. *Jīva* performs an action only under some situation, pleasant or painful, which is given to it. This goes on ad infinitum. Now the question

---

[2] *kāyavāṅmanaḥ karma yogaḥ* । – *Tattvārthasūtra* 6.1

arises; if *jīva* has been in bondage without beginning, will it continue to be so without an end? Is freedom from bondage possible? If so, how is it possible?

THE POSSIBILITY OF LIBERATION

On this issue, Jains hold that though *jīva* is in bondage without beginning, it is not because it essentially exists as such. The essence of *jīva* is not to be in bondage but to have infinite capacity for intuition, knowledge, bliss and energy.[3] These four infinities, which constitute the very essence of *jīva*, are obscured due to various kinds of *karmas*. There are four kinds of *karmas* which directly obstruct these infinite capacities and hence they are called *ghātī-karmas*. They are intuition-obscuring (*darśanāvaraṇīya*), knowledge-obscuring (*jñānāvaraṇīya*), deluding (*mohanīya*) and impending (*antarāya*) *karmas* (*Gommaṭasāra-Karmakāṇḍa* 9). *Jīva* can experience intuition, knowledge, bliss or energy when the respective *karma* is destroyed or has subsided. It can be liberated by destroying all *karmas* completely. The path of the destruction of these *karmas* is the Jain path of self-purification.

Jains believe that the liberated state of *jīva* exists in three forms. The first one is called the state of *sayoga-kevalī* (embodied liberation), the second is called the state of *ayoga-kevalī* (disembodied liberation) and the third one is called the state of *siddha* (accomplished one). In the first state, *jīva* is free from all the obstructive *karmas* and hence it realizes all the four infinities, but the non-obstructive *karmas* (*aghātī-karmas*) still remain due to which *jīva* continues to live in embodied form. There are four non-obstructive *karmas* acknowledged by Jains:

1. the sensation-determining *karma* (*vedanīya karma*), which causes pleasant and painful sensations,
2. the life-determining *karma* (*āyu-karma*), which determines the span of life,

---

[3] *jñānadarśanadānalābhabhogopabhogavīryāṇi ca* । – *Tattvārthasūtra* 2.4

3. the physique-making *karma* (*nāma-karma*), which determines various physiological features, and
4. the status-determining *karma* (*gotra-karma*), which determines the social position or status.

Due to these *karmas*, *sayoga-kevalī* lives the full span of its life performing various actions and experiencing pleasant and unpleasant sensations. But since he performs actions without any passions, no new kārmic matter sticks to him. When the non-obstructive *karmas* are exhausted, such a person dies and attains the second state of liberation; the state of *ayoga-kevalī*. In this state, *jīva* becomes fully disembodied, goes upward, up to the end of the universe-space (i.e. non-empty space) and stays there permanently. *Jīva* in this paramount state is called *siddha* (*Gommaṭasāra-Jīvakāṇḍa* 63-68).

From the moral point of view, *sayoga-kevalī* is more important because in this state the embodied *jīva*, which is still a person, performs various actions, experiences pleasant and unpleasant sensations, and yet he is free because he does not develop any passions towards these actions and sensations. But how does *jīva* attain freedom from passions? How does he step onto the path of self-purification?

The Path of the Three Jewels

The purification of the soul is achieved through the path of the three jewels. These three jewels are: *samyak-darśana* (right belief), *samyak-jñāna* (right knowledge) and *samyak-cāritra* (right conduct).[4] *Samyak-darśana* is defined by Umāsvāti as the faith in the basic tenets (of Jainism).[5] *Samyak-jñāna* is understood as intellectual knowledge of the basic tenets (Sogani 1967: 184). These two jewels, viz. right faith and right knowledge, are supposed to form the basis of the right conduct. Ultimately, it is the right conduct that will liberate *jīva*

---

[4] *samyagdarśanajñānacāritrāṇi mikṣamārgaḥ* । – *Tattvārthasūtra* 1.1

[5] *tattvārthaśraddhānaṁ samyagdarśanaṁ* । – ibid. 1.2

(Bhargava 1968: 83). Hence, unlike many other schools of Indian philosophy, classical Jainism does not regard self-knowledge as the ultimate liberating factor, but regards right conduct based on right faith and right knowledge to be so (Bhargava 1968: 96-97).

The Jain concept of right conduct is not that of moral conduct in the ordinary sense of the term, but the conduct which amounts to the stoppage of the inflow of *karma* particles and the eradication of the already existing *karma* particles, which have bound the soul. Accordingly, the concept of right conduct has both moral and spiritual aspects.

RIGHT CONDUCT

The notion of right conduct has been variously elaborated in Jainism. Primarily, it is articulated through the conception of *vrata* (vow, restraint) which is further classified into various kinds, the five basic ones being: *ahiṁsā* (non-violence), *satya* (truthfulness), *asteya* (non-stealing), *brahmacarya* (celibacy) and *aparigraha* (non-possession). They are supposed to be followed by the Jain ascetics (*śramaṇas*) in a very rigorous way. The same vows are to be followed by lay-followers also, but since the latter are supposed to have social and familial responsibilities and as they are also susceptible to temptations and passions of various kinds, they cannot follow the vows with the same rigour as the ascetics supposed to do. Hence, the content and intensity of the vows are moderated for them. The five basic vows which are to be followed by the ascetics are called *mahāvrata* (great vows), whereas the same to be followed by the laity are called *aṇuvrata* (minor vows) (*Tattvārthasāra* 4.60-61).

In Jain literature, we find a detailed explanation of these vows with the transgressions (*aticāra*) to be avoided, whose practice is to be perfected. The practice of the small vows is supposed to be strengthened further in the laity by the practice of *guṇa vrata*s (supplementary vows) and *śikṣā vrata*s (vows of training) (ibid. 4.81). Similarly, the practice of great vows is supposed to be strengthened in the monks by following the rules of *samiti* (carefulness) and *gupti* (protection). It is supposed to be supplemented further by different kinds of tolerances (*parīṣahajaya*; literally, conquering the endurables) and contemplations (*anuprekṣā*).[6]

RECONSTRUCTION OF RIGHT CONDUCT

The Jain conception of *samyak-cāritra* is not available to us always in a consistent and systematic form. *Saṁvara*, *nirjarā* and *cāritra* are known to overlap with each other. Umāsvāti[7] and others, for instance, divide *bhava-saṁvara* (mental aspect of the stoppage of the kārmic matter inflow) into seven parts: *vrata*, *samiti*, *gupti*, *dharma* (teaching), *anuprekṣā*, *parīṣahajaya* and *cāritra*. Out of them, *dharma* includes *satya*, *tapas* (penance) and *brahmacarya*, but *satya* and *brahmacarya* are also included in *vrata*.

Hence, the concepts of *vrata* and *dharma* overlap. Similarly, *tapas* is an important way to *nirjarā*, but here it is included in *saṁvara*. Hence, the distinction between *saṁvara* and *nirjarā* does not seem to be sharp. In the above division, *cāritra* is separated from *vrata*, *samiti* and *gupti*, but we also find that *samyak-cāritra* is explained in terms of the same three principles. In some places, the term *dharma* is used in the same sense as *cāritra*. Yet, according to a commentarial text, the *Sūtrakr̥tāṅgavr̥tti*, *dharma* consists of *ahiṁsā* and *parīṣahajaya*. Here, the scope of *dharma* seems to be narrower than that of *cāritra*.

Another point worth noting here is that *samyak-cāritra* is generally not applied to the conduct of householders but to that of monks. Thus, it includes *mahāvratas* only. The complex situation indicated above underlines the need for reconstruction and rearrangement of the principles in Jainism concerning right conduct. Here, the following rearrangement of the terms concerning right conduct is suggested. Instead of *cāritra*, *ācāra* is the

---

[6] *sa gupti samiti dharmānuprekṣā pariṣahajaya cāritraiḥ* ।
– *Tattvārthasūtra* 9.1

[7] See *Tattvārthasūtra*, chap. 9.

first broad category which covers the code of conduct for the laity (*śrāvakācāra*) and that for the monks (*śramaṇācāra*). Out of them, the former has already been classified into *aṇuvratas*, *guṇa vratas* and *śikṣā vratas*, though the last two sometimes overlap with each other. The code of conduct for monks can be identified as *samyak-cāritra*.

Different aspects of *samyak-cāritra* seem to overlap with each other, but a rearrangement of these aspects is possible by which such admixtures are minimized. Hence, the principles of conduct coming under *samyak-cāritra* could be broadly classified into two types – those involving abstentions which amount to avoiding or stopping the inflow of *karma-pudgalas* (*saṁvara*) and those involving special purificatory activities which amount to purging the soul of the *karma-pudgalas* (*avipāka-nirjarā*). Accordingly, *vrata*, *samiti* and *gupti* amount to abstaining from violence, untruth and possession in a vigilant and careful way, and thereby protecting one's soul from kārmic inflections. Hence, these principles belong to the first type of *samyak-cāritra*. On the other hand, the acts like *anuprekṣā*, *tapas*, *parīṣahajaya* and *sāmāyika* (developing equanimity) are not abstentions, but positive purificatory acts. In this way, *saṁvara* and *nirjarā* (purgation of *karma*-matter) gives one the principle of the classification of right conduct.

Issues Concerning Jain Ethics and Ahiṁsā

MORALITY AND SPIRITUALITY

Ethical conduct in some form is a necessary condition of liberation. Thus, one can be sceptical about this view. One can point out here the distinction made by Umāsvāti[8] between two paths of action: *īryāpatha* (non-binding path) and *sāmparāyika* (transmigrational path). The transmigrational action is of two kinds: *śubha* and *aśubha* (auspicious and inauspicious) both of which cause bondage. Hence, if *śubha* action is understood as moral action, then one will have to admit that morality does not lead to liberation but to bondage.

[8] See *Tattvārthasūtra*, chap. 6.

On the other hand, what is important for liberation is that actions should be free from passions (*akaṣāya-yoga*). *Īryāpatha* type of action is supposed to be non-binding because it is free from passions. This account of binding and non-binding action given by Umāsvāti dissociates morality from spirituality. But this account leads to two problems:

1. Umāsvāti defines *yoga* as bodily, vocal and mental action, and identifies it with *āsrava*. Yet, *āsrava* is so-called because it amounts to the inflow of kārmic matter. This implies that every action, whether bodily, vocal or mental, leads to bondage. However, by introducing the notion of passionless action, Umāsvāti points out that a non-binding action is possible. Therein lies the first inconsistency.
2. Umāsvāti's account suggests that passions (*kaṣāyas*) are detrimental to spiritual emancipation, but they are morally neutral because both immoral and moral actions contain passions. But are passions really morally neutral? One can argue that they are not. For instance, anger is one of the passions and when it itself amounts to mental *hiṁsā* or a cause of *hiṁsā*. Freedom from anger amounts to a large extent to freedom from *hiṁsā*. Now, avoiding *hiṁsā* is a *śubha-yoga* (an auspicious action) and also a vow leading to liberation. Hence, the ideas of moral action and non-binding action overlap. It is possible that Umāsvāti, while talking about *śubha-āsrava*, is describing the auspicious actions performed out of passions or quasi-passions (*kaṣāyas* or *no-kaṣāyas*). For instance, one may do charity to poor people out for greed for popularity, pride or fear (guilty feeling). But one can perhaps say that such actions are not fully moral in the strict sense of the term, because the motive behind them is not moral – they are not performed out of pure and simple good will.

In this sense, passions and quasi-passions (at least some of them) could be regarded not only as spiritual deficiencies but also moral deficiencies. They are not only detrimental to liberation but also to moral perfection. Similarly, elimination of passions not only leads to spiritual perfection, but also to moral perfection (in the form of practising *ahiṁsā* and other moral values in their fullest possible extent). Thus, morality and spirituality are closely interrelated in Jain philosophy.

References

Ācārya Nemicandra, 1999, *Gommaṭasāra-Karmakāṇḍa*, ed. A.N. Shastri, New Delhi: Bharatiya Jnanpith.

——, 2004, *Gommaṭasāra-Jīvakāṇḍa*, vol. I, ed. A.N. Shastri, New Delhi: Bharatiya Jnanpith.

Ācāya Pūjyapāda, 1997, *Sarvārthasiddhi*, ed. P. Shastri, New Delhi: Bharatiya Jnanpith.

Amṛtacandra Sūri, 1970, *Tattvārthasāra*, Varanasi: Shri Ganeshprasad Varni Granthamala.

Bhargava, D.N., 1968, *Jain Ethics*, Delhi: Motilal Banarsidass.

Sogani, K.C., 1967, *Ethical Doctrines in Jainism*. Solapur: Lalchand Hirachand Joshi Jain Sanskriti Sanrakshak Sangh.

Umāsvāti, 2009, *Tattvārthasūtra*, ed. S. Sanhvi, Varanasi: Parshvanath Vidyapeeth.

8

Niyativāda as Depicted in Jainism

Navin K. Srivastav

The Śramaṇic tradition, as well as the Vedic tradition, emphasized Niyativāda from their own particular perspective to explain the theory of causation. The specific meaning of *niyati* is the "deliberate hiding of the truth". The word *niyati* stands for fate, the mysterious but irresistible power of the acts done in previous lives, which rules unnoticed in the present life. Niyativāda or Daivavāda is, therefore, the doctrine of fatalism, pre-destination, all-embracing, overmastering fate, a mysterious cosmic power which controls every action and phenomenon in this universe. This doctrine leaves no scope for human effort or free will as it regards *niyati*, as the only determining factor of the universe and the sole agent of all changes. By this ruling principle of the cosmic process, all things occur in a pre-determined pattern.

Niyativāda proper finds no place in orthodox Hinduism, Buddhism and Jainism. A man's fortune, his social status and his happiness or grief are all ultimately due to his own free will. The Indian doctrine of *karma* provides a rigid framework within which the individual is able to move freely and to act on his own decision, as it is usually interpreted. His present condition is determined not by any immutable principle, but by his own actions performed either in this life or in his past lives. By freely choosing the right course and following it, he may improve his lot and ultimately win salvation either by his own unassisted efforts, or, if he is a member of a devotional sect, with the aid of a personal deity.

The doctrine of free will was opposed by Makkhali Gośālaka,[1] a contemporary of Tīrthaṅkara Mahāvīra and Gautama Buddha. Gośālaka and his Niyativāda were extremely popular, as seen from the Buddhist and Jain attacks on them. According to the Buddhist (*Dīgha Nikāya–Samaññaphala Sutta*) and Jain sources (*Bhagavatīsutra* 15th *śataka*), Ājīvakas, the sect founded by Gośālaka, believed in fate rather than *karma*. The Ājīvikas believed that transmigration of the human soul was determined by a precise and non-personal cosmic principle called *niyati* that was completely independent of the person's actions. Gośālaka said to have believed that the suffering and evil experienced by a being came not from his previous *karma* but from the fate to which he was subject. The Ājīvikas discounted all human effort; everything came out of fate and nothing could be done to change it. Thus, there was no use fighting against it. They believed that the number of souls was infinite and in the reincarnation of souls and the cycles of creation. According to some versions, the Ājīvikas were an atheistic sect. However, it is possible that the Ājīvikas actually believed in the will of God,

---

[1] The *Bhagavatīsūtra* (one of the Jain canons) states that Gośālaka became Mahāvīra's disciple three years after the start of Mahāvīra's asceticism, and travelled with him for the next six years. A commentary to the Jain *Āvaśyakasūtra* provides details of these six years of association, many of them reflecting poorly on Gośālaka – another likely indication of sectarian bias. Several incidents in the narrative show Mahāvīra making predictions that then come true, despite Gośālaka repeated attempts to foil them. These incidents were likely included in the narrative to provide motivation for Gośālaka's later belief in the inevitability of fate. Some of these incidents may in fact have been adapted from Ājīvika sources but recast by Jain chroniclers.

which in this case is synonymous with fate and surrendered to it without question. Since Buddhism and Jainism did not believe in the existence of absolute God, nor in any divine design hidden in creation or the unfolding of life, they might have interpreted the beliefs and practices of Ājīvakas as fatalistic to prove their point.

The Jain tradition, as well as all Śramaṇic traditions, refute fatalism as accepted by Ājīvikas in their own particular form. According to the Jain doctrine of *karma*, an individual's present condition is determined not by any absolute principle but by his own actions performed either in the past lives; by freely choosing the right course and following it faithfully he could improve his destiny and ultimately win salvation.

Yet, the scholars' refutation of the doctrine of *niyati* should not lead us to conclude that they totally reject that doctrine. There are so many examples in Jain literature, where the author accepted Niyativāda. Siddhasena Divākara (fifth century CE), one of the great logicians, proposes in the *Sanmatitarka* five theories of causation: *kāla* (time), *svabhāva* (nature), *niyati* (determinism), *pūrvakṛta adṛṣṭa* (chance accident) and *puruṣārtha* (effort).[2] If all these five theories are taken singly, they are false because they touch only one point. These all are true when they are made use of with reference to each other. Thus, *niyati* is of equal importance as compared to the rest of the theories of causation.

As the origination of a new event is due to a cause, many schools of thought on causation have arisen. Five of them are:

1. Kālavādī, who take time to be the only cause and argue out that different types of fruits are due to winter, summer and monsoon, and the *ṛtu-bheda* (change in season) is nothing but *kāla-viśeṣa* (particular change of time).

---

[2] *kālosahāvaṇiyaīpuvvakayaṁpurisekāraṇeṅgatā* ।
micchattaṁtecevasamāsaohoṁtisammattaṁ ।।
– *Sanmatitarka Prakaraṇa* 3.53

2. Svabhāvavādī, who regard *svabhāva* (nature) as the only cause. Their central argument is that the walking capacity of the animals only in land, flying power of the birds in the sky, tenderness of fruits and the pointedness of a thorn are all due to nothing but their inherent nature.
3. Niyativādī, whose theory is that destiny only is the cause. They believe that which is to be obtained, shall be obtained; what is to happen, will happen, what is not to occur, shall never come to pass. All this is due to fate; time and nature have nothing to do with it.
4. Adṛṣṭavādī, who think that *adṛṣṭa* only is the cause. All humans are born with *karma* done in their past births and they are taken into the kārmic current unexpectedly. Man's intellect is not independent; it shapes its course according to the *karmas* accumulated, thus *adṛṣṭa* only in the cause of all.
5. Puruṣārthavādī, who advocate that *puruṣa* only is the cause. In support of their theory, they argue that God creates, destroys and keeps this world stable, just as a spider weaves a web and a tree shoots forth sprouts. They support no argument outside God. This is *īśvara-tantra*, a government of God. Everything is done by *puruṣa* and the concept that God is within us.

This causal theory is also put forth in Haribhadrasūri's (eighth century CE) *Viṁśati-viṁśikā Prakaraṇam*; all five theories are true if they are made use of with reference to each other and they have the possibility to solve the faced problem.[3] Vedic texts, such as the *Śvetāśvatara Upaniṣad*, also mention clearly the various theories of causation: *kāla, svabhāva, niyati, yadṛcchā* (chance accident), *bhūtāni*

[3] *kālosahāvaṇiyaīpuvvakayaṁpurisakāraṇegantāṁ* ।
micchantaṁteceva u samāsaohotisammataṁ ।।
– *Viṁśati-Viṁśikā Prakaraṇam* 4.14

(elements) and *puruṣa* (supreme, highest person).[4]

Incidentally, it may be inferred that *niyati*, as interpreted by Gośālaka, means the invisible, overmastering cosmic power destiny. It may also stand for one's own destiny, the sum total of past good and bad deeds performed by individuals. The principles of Niyativāda, as advocated by Gośālaka, are clearly embodied in the *Uvāsagadasāo* which explains:

> There was no such thing as exertion or labour or power or energy or human strength, and that all things are unalterably fixed.
>
> – Sikdar 1964: 440[5]

Gośālaka's doctrine effectively means that both, the sinner and the saint, the fool and the wise, are on equal footing as far as the winning of ultimate liberation is concerned. A more clear conception of determinism is found in Buddhist works, such as the *Dīgha Nikāya*, where it is stated:

> There is no cause either proximate or remote for the purity of beings: they become pure without reason or cause. Nothing depends either on one's own effort or on the efforts of others [...] everything that lives is destitute of force, power or energy. These varying conditions at any time are due to fate [...] that men experience ease or pain. Likewise, the escape from evil, the working off of accumulated evil *karma* was without cause or basis – *ahetu-apaccayosattāvisujhanti.* – Ibid.: 441

The doctrine turns out to be predominantly pessimistic, whereas the doctrine of *karma* brings some comfort and solace to a man in distress and operates as a guideline of moral conduct to improve

---

4 *kalaḥ svabhāvo niyatiryadr̥cchā bhūtāni yoniḥ puruṣa iti cintyam* ।
saṁyoga eṣāṁ na tvātmabhāvādātmāpyanīśaḥ sukhaduḥ khahetoḥ ।।
– *Śvetāśvatara Upaniṣad* 1.2

5 *ta eṇaṁ se saddalaputtaājīviovāsa esa maṇaṁbhagavaṁ mahāvīraṁ evaṁ vayāsī-bhante! aṇuṭṭhāṇeṇaṁ java apurisakkāra-parakkameṇaṁ* । *natthiuṭṭhāṇeivā java parakkameivā, niyayāsavvabhāvā* ।।
– *Upāsaka-daśāṅgasūtra* 7.199

his destiny and win his salvation by his own efforts; it is full of optimism and conducive to soul, morality and good conduct.

Determinism, Indeterminism and Freedom

If the relation between the soul and *karmas* is designated as interactionism, in which neither the substances nor the attributes of the one are transformed into those of the others, the same is the limitation when *karma* is said to determine the physiology and the environment connected with *jīva*. The theory of *karma* is in Indian philosophy as well as Jain philosophical perspective, the soul is to be bound with its own actions, which is not transformed to others. The *karma* becomes simply an occasion, or *nimittakāraṇa*, in the determinism of the psychic, psychological and environmental variations. Under these limitations, *karma*-determinism can simply mean an agreement between the potency of the *karma* and the consequent variation in the above-mentioned three spheres.

Samantabhadra objects to absolute *karma*-determinism as:

> if things are accomplished solely by the fate (or *karmas*), then it cannot maintain that fate can also be determined by *puruṣārtha*. If fate is determined by another fate, then emancipation becomes impossible and effort fruitless.[6]

Samantabhadara also states:

> If it is maintained that all attainment of objects is due to determination, then the question arises how it sometimes happens that the fate creates determination. And if it is replied that determination is always a creation of determination it follows that the endeavour of people should always prove a success.[7]

---

[6] *daivādevārthasiddhiścеddaivaṁpauruṣataḥ katham* ।
daivataścedanirmokṣaḥ pauruṣaṁ niṣphalaṁbhavet ।।
– *Āptamīmāṁsā*, 88

[7] *pauruṣādevasiddhiścetpauruṣaṁdaivataḥkatham* ।
pauruṣāccedamoghaṃsyātsarvaprāṇiṣupauruṣam ।।
– Ibid. 89

If we accept *niyati*, there is no scope for self-effort. Yet, we cannot go to the other extreme of absolute indeterminism and hold that it will be perfectly independent of kārmic influence. The absolutism of indeterminism also leads to the futility of the *karma* doctrine. If *karmas* have no bearing on the behaviour of living beings, they are as good as non-existent. Samantabhadra again observes; if things are accomplished by effort only, effort cannot be determined by *karma* or fate. If fate is then determined solely by effort, then effort will become fruitful in the case of all living beings. Yet, no living being is absolutely free to choose and act. Such a limitation is felt by every individual and it speaks to the truth of kārmic influence.

The concept of freedom or indeterminism may be taken to yield two meanings: first, it may stand for creating a situation which balances the effect of the *karmas*. *Karmas* alone cannot yield something which is detrimental to one's own working. Hence, this effort must be due to the soul itself; it is on account of its own powers that it is able to maintain itself against the *karmas*. The freedom of the soul may be held to lie in this maintenance. Second, freedom finds its full meaning only in the destructive type of conscious manifestations, *kṣāyika*. Such a manifestation is determined by the soul itself, and hence, it may be termed as free. "Determinism in the sense of self-determination is not inconsistent with freedom", as Rashdall holds (1907: 309). Absolute freedom, as distinct from self-determinism, is a meaningless conception. Many writers have supposed themselves to be defending indeterminism when they were really determinists themselves in the sense of self-determinism. Still more have been so understood by readers not unwilling to be deceived. Many Jain scholars, like Samantabhadra, Haribhadra, Jain canons (*Sūtrakṛtāṅga*) and many Western idealist scholars, like St. Thomas Aquinas, Georg Wilhelm Friedrich Hegel and T.H. Green, have often been taken for indeterminists or defenders of free will in the popular sense (Dixit 2002: 164-93).

The conception of time, nature, determinism, chance-accident and self-effort cannot be thought separately, they mutually imply each other. It is said:

> The liberty with effort subjugated by time and necessity both cooperate symphonically in the production of every human thought. Every human life and the conduct therefore are but reconciliation between liberty and necessity.
>
> – Nahar and Ghosh 1917: 384

Not only freedom presupposes determinism, but the reserve is also true. It is true because determinism and freedom are very closely associated with the personality of living beings. In terms of Jain philosophy, moral accountability may be interpreted as a liability for bondage. Yet, this bondage does not take place totally, according to the operation of the *karmas*. Siddhasena and Haribhadrasūri quoted above discussed that these doctrines as the first cause of the universe are false when they are taken singly, but they are true when they are accommodated, adjusted and related to each other in accordance with their well-known doctrine of Syādvāda and Anekāntavāda.

References

Ācārya Haribhadra, 1932, *Viṁśati-Viṁśikā*, ed. K.V. Abhyankar, Pune: Aryabhushan Mudranalay.

Ācārya Samantabhadra, 2016, *Āptamīmāṁsā*, tr. V.K. Jain, Dehradun: Vikalp Printers.

Divākara, S., 1939, *Sanmati-Tarka*, ed. D. Malavania, Bombay: Shri Jain Shwetambar Education Board.

Dixit, K.K., 2002, *Śāstra-vārtā-samuccaya of Haribhadra Sūri*, Ahmedabad: L.D. Institute of Indology.

Madhukar Muni (ed.), 2006, *Upāsaka-daśāṅgasūtra*, Beawar: Shri Agam Prakashan Samiti.

Nahar, P.C. and K.C. Ghosh, 1917, *An Epitome of Jainism: Being a Critical Study of Its Metaphysics, Ethics, and History, etc. in Relation to Modern Thought*, Calcutta: H. Dubey Publication.

Rashdall, H., 1907, *The Theory of Good and Evil*, vol. II, Oxford: Clarendon Press.

Sikdar, J.C., 1964, *Studies in Bhagwati Sutra*, vol. I, Muzaffarpur: Research Institute of Prakrit, Jainology and Ahimsa.

Śvetāśvatara Upaniṣad, M. Giri, Varanasi: Shri Dakshinamurti Math Prakashan, 1975.

9

Determinism, Free Will and Morality

A Jain Perspective

Jinesh R. Sheth

THE problem of determinism and free will has occupied the minds of philosophers for centuries. From one side, it is argued that since all the actions are causally determined, the belief that one is free is an illusion; from the other side, it is argued that since one knows that one is free and that one could have acted otherwise, universal determinism is false. The problem of moral responsibility is another issue that requires separate treatment.

Omniscience and determinism (Niyativāda) are related in such a way that the former logically implies the latter, though it may not be vice versa. The answer to whether the Jain thinkers agree with determinism would be positive, given the fact that omniscience is strongly defended by them.[1] The task at hand is to then look for the

[1] Jainism, as a system, is based on the teachings of the omniscient being. It is but obvious that the very possibility of omniscience and its presence in the *arhats* needs to be thus proved rigorously. This also justifies it being called an exegetical school, though not exclusively. The *Pravacanasāra* (Book I) of Ācārya Kundakunda was perhaps the first philosophical text in the tradition to give a proof of omniscience. Later on, Ācārya →

consistency amongst the three – determinism, free will and moral responsibility – within the theoretical framework provided by the Jains. Accounting for this consistency is one amongst the many unresolved problems in philosophy even today, which is what will be undertaken in this paper.

The paper is divided into three parts – the first part deals with the Jain account of Niyativāda with reference to its position on omniscience, *karma* and *paryāya*. The second part discusses free will and how Jain thinkers are able to accommodate both determinism and free will. The third part will then talk of moral responsibility in line with the above two.

Niyativāda in Relation to Omniscience, Karma and Paryāya

Determinism is a philosophical position according to which all events are certain and that nothing can prevent them from happening at that particular instance of time. Due to diverse motives and considerations, there have been many versions of deterministic theories in the philosophical tradition – ontological, theological, physical, logical, psychological and ethical.

← Samantabhadra's *Āptamīmāṁsā* was another significant text wherein arguments are found for the possibility of omniscience, in general, and its existence in *arhats*, in particular (vv. 5-6). Moreover, the commentaries of Akalaṅkadeva and Vidyānanda, viz. the *Aṣṭaśatī* and *Aṣṭasahasrī*, especially the latter, discussed at length omniscience while commenting on those verses. Ācārya Prabhācandra, in his *Prameyakamalamārtaṇḍa*, a commentary on Ācārya Māṇikyanandi's *Parīkṣāmukham*, offered as well quite a few interesting arguments for omniscience while discussing about *mukhya pratyakṣa* in the second chapter. Ācārya Malliṣenasūri, in his *Syādvāda Mañjarī*, also deals with the problem in the commentary on the first verse (see Ācārya Malliṣeṇasūri 1968). The list is endless and it is clearly evident how important this doctrine has been to Jain thinkers throughout history. For a more detailed study on the Jain notion of omniscience, arguments for its existence and some debates with other philosophical systems (see Singh 1974).

Against any form of determinism, the general argument which is put forth is summed up in the "idle argument" which was articulated by Greek thinkers. According to Diodorus, there is no point in any man's taking of any precautions or making preparation. The argument runs as follows: if, for instance, a man is ill, then it follows from Diodorus's principle, that he is either going to recover or he is not going to recover. If he is going to recover, then he will eventually recover whether or not he summons a physician; similarly, if he is going to perish, then he will perish whether or not he summons a physician. Hence, there is no point in his summoning a physician in either case because the outcome is already inevitable. However, Chrysippus came up with a brilliant reply with the theory of co-destined facts – facts whose truths are dependent upon one another (Taylor 2006: 6).

Thus, there is not only a temporal precedence of one cause over the other but also a logical connection between them. It also implies that there can be multiple causes in origination of one particular event. So, if the man is going to recover, it is also fated that he will see a physician and if he is going to perish, it is also fated that he will fail to see a physician.

The fivefold causal theory (*pañca-samavāya*) speaks exactly in similar fashion – an event or an effect always has multiple causes which are mutually dependent on each other for their being true. Ācārya Siddhasena discusses about them in his *Sanmatitarka Prakaraṇa*:

> To exclusively consider only one of the five – time, nature, destiny, instrument and effort – as the cause of the origination of an event is a perverse belief and to regard the mass of all those as the cause of origination of an event is right belief.[2]

---

[2] *kālo sahāva ṇiyaī puvvakayaṁ purisakāraṇegaṁtā* ।
micchattaṁ te ceva u samāsao hoṁti sammattaṁ ।।
– *Sanmatitarka Prakaraṇa* 3.53

Amongst these five, the instrumental cause is extrinsic in nature, while the remaining four are intrinsic or inherent in nature. A cause will be called a cause if and only if it is in harmony with the other four and thereby leading to a particular effect. There might be a difference of emphasis since all cannot be accounted together, a limitation of language, but none can be disregarded. Thus, even though *niyati* is one amongst many causes leading to the origination of an event, so is *puruṣārtha.*

Two of these will now be examined further from the Jain perspective in a theological manner, with reference to omniscience and in a metaphysical manner, with reference to *karma* and *paryāya.*

Theological Determinism

Omniscience, as defined in the *Tattvārthasūtra*, refers to the knowledge of all the substances and their modifications – past, present and future.[3] The fact that future events are foreknown by the omniscient being implies unconditionally that they are not contingent; for they could have been known if and only if they were certain. This entailment, however, does not imply that the future events are caused by the omniscient being's ability to know them. Neither the knowledge of the omniscient being is seen as a prediction of events; nor is it the case that the omniscient being wills for some particular events to happen in future. Both are independent of each other and as the saying goes – a sign shows that to which it points without thereby producing it; knowledge of an event thus cannot be the cause of its occurrence. Yet, there still remains a logical connection between the knowledge of future events and their being certain. Therefore, even if foreknowledge is not the cause of those things that are foreknown, it nonetheless renders them certainty and thereby the inevitability. The argument goes as follows:

a. An omniscient being, say *A*, foreknows that *S* will do *P* at a particular instance of time.

[3] *sarvadravyaparyāyeṣu kevalasya* । – *Tattvārthasūtra* 1.30

b. For *A*'s knowledge to be true, it is necessary that *S* must do *P* at that particular instance of time.
c. If *S* does not do *P*, it follows that *A*'s knowledge that *S* will do *P* is false and hence *A* is not an omniscient being.
d. And, if it is granted that *A* is an omniscient being, it inevitably follows that the future events are also determined and will inevitably occur at those particular instances of time.

As Taylor says:

> The extension of this [omniscience] thought to all actions of all men leads quite naturally to the view that no man's action is ever free or that nothing any man ever does was avoidable, it having always been true that he was going to do what he eventually did.
>
> – 2006: 6

Although this argument may not prove omniscience itself, it does prove that if omniscience is granted, determinism is a necessary corollary of it. We may refer to it as theological determinism, as it is based on divine omniscience. Whether such type of determinism is "soft" or "hard" and whether it issues any threats to free will are some other questions which will be discussed in the second section.

Metaphysical Determinism

There are two notions through which determinism will be discussed – one is *karma* and the other one is that of *paryāya* (modification of a substance).[4]

In the *karma* theory, unlike the other systems where it is usually seen as a law of moral retribution, it must be noted that, here, *karma*

[4] According to Jainism, everything that is real must have the triple character of origination, cessation and, at the same time, continuity or persistence. And that which lacks one or the other cannot be termed as real. The former two constitute the changing aspect of reality, whereas continuity is an aspect representing permanence and thus the position permanence-cum-change. – *Tattvārthasūtra* 5.29

is conceived as a physical matter.[5] The *siddhas* have become free from all types of *karmas* and, hence, they are not subject to any kārmic fruition. One must remember that *karma* is an extrinsic cause amongst the five causes that we had discussed earlier. Nevertheless, it still has a strong influence on the actions of the soul and whether it will attain liberation, for *mokṣa* is defined as "an absence of the causes of bondage and on account of *nirjarā* there takes place an utter annihilation of *karmas*. The annihilation of all *karmas* - that is called *mokṣa*" (Dixit, 2000: 56). The *karma* theory, on one hand, can lead to a straightforward causal determinism given the fact that each and every action of the soul is an outcome of the fruition of past *karma*; whereas, on the other hand, due to its own subtleties and various nuances, one can also entail that it does not lead to complete fatalism.

The Jain thinkers have systematized the *karma* doctrine to such an extent that it is possible for them to account for every disposition in a soul with its corresponding *karma*, albeit with one exception, *jñāna*.[6] So whether it is the soul's attainment of the three jewels; miserable suffering in the world while going from one phase of life to another; or any other activity – in all of them, *karma* plays a vital role.

Coming to the notion of *paryāya*, which represents the

---

[5] For a discussion and some good arguments on how something physical can make an impact on something which is not, see Todarmal 2005: pp. 32-33.

[6] Amongst the five *bhāvas* mentioned in *Tattvārthasūtra* 2.1, only the fifth one, *pāriṇāmika bhāva*, is unrelated to *karma;* whereas all other *bhāvas* exactly correspond to the four types (and also sub-types) of *ghāti-karma* (those which directly affect the soul). There is a difference between an ability to know and knowledge itself. Although there is one *karma* known as *jñānāvaraṇa*, it is related to how much a soul can know and not to whether it can know at all; for it is the differentia of the soul and it is quite obvious that it is not subjected to any kind of *karma*.

changing aspect of reality, there is a scope for determinism which is neither theological nor causal. The origination and cessation of a modification happening at every instance of time is in a particular sequence which is determined by the thing itself. The substance cannot be without a modification for any given instance nor is it the case that a new modification originates without the destruction of the previous one. However, the change cannot be so radical that a *jīva* will get transformed into an *ajīva*. As said by Amṛtacandra in his commentary of v. 308[7] in the *Samayasāra*:

> Whatever is produced by the direct self-manifestation of *jīva*, the living being, is also of the nature of living being, and cannot be a non-living thing. In the same manner, whatever is produced by the direct manifestation of the non-living material must also be of the nature of the non-living material, and cannot certainly be of the nature of living being. – Chakravarty 2008: 414-15

The term *kaṇayamaṇaṇṇamiha* (*kramaniyamita*) suggests that the sequence of modifications cannot occur by chance. This is again proved by Amṛtacandra in his commentary on one of the verses in the *Pravacanasāra* with the example of a necklace:

> As in the case of a hanging necklace of pearls, of definite length, the threefoldness [origination, destruction and stability] is obvious, because, whilst all the pearls are visible each in its place, each subsequent pearl arises (before our perception) in a subsequent place, each precedent pearl does not arise in the subsequent place, [and] the whole necklace, which strings-them-together by means of a mutual stringing together, is present in all their places; in the same manner in the case of a substance, developing with definite eternal activity (*vṛtti*), the threefoldness is obvious, because, whilst all the evolutions are visible each in its own point-of-time, each subsequent evolution arises in a subsequent point-of-time, each precedent evolution does not

[7] *daviyaṁ jaṁ uppajjadi guṇehi taṁ tehi jāṇasu aṇaṇṇaṁ* ।
jaha kaḍayādīhiṁ du ya pajjaehi kaṇayamaṇaṇṇamih ।। – *Samayasāra* 308

> arise in the subsequent point-of-time, [and] the whole process (*pravāha*) which strings-them-together by means of a mutual stringing together, is present in all their points-of-time.
>
> – Thomas 2014: 74-75

It is clear that each modification in its own time is born in its own shape, destroys its own previous form and continuity of modifications being there, every modification retains its own shape. From the example of the necklace of pearls, just as the location of the pearls is fixed in the necklace, the time of appearance of the pearls in the looming necklace is also fixed. Every modification takes place in its time only.[8]

Coexistence of Free Will and Determinism in Jainism

It is generally observed that any form of determinism poses challenge to the doctrine of free will, the capacity of rational agents to choose a course of action among various alternatives (O'Connor 2002). Much of the debate about free will revolves around whether we have it. It also depends on how one defines freedom. Philosophers are widely divided over which sort of action could be called "free" and they have debated over this question for about two millennia and almost every major philosopher had something to say about it (ibid.).

Free will cannot be always equated with the statement that the person is free if and only if he could have acted otherwise; this phrase is rather misleading and deceptive. Although it has been argued that "he could have acted otherwise" is inconsistent with determinism, one must reconsider the very notion of freedom itself. As Taylor (2006: 11-12) points out:

> Hobbes dismissed the question whether men's wills are free as "improper" or meaningless. Generations of philosophers, while for the most part rejecting Hobbes's materialism, have nevertheless followed him in this and in his conception of liberty.

---

[8] For a more detailed account on this, see Jain 1987: 36-39.

> His concept of free and voluntary behaviour is nothing but an unconstrained and unimpeded behaviour that is caused by an act of will, a motive, or some other inner event. In the twentieth century, Moritz Schlick, A.J. Ayer, and many others made the point that freedom is not opposed to causation but to constraint.

In the Indian tradition, although both the elements – fate and perseverance – have been recognized, it is not articulated in the form of a philosophical problem for some unknown reasons. In Jainism, Samantabhadra was perhaps the first one to explicitly deal with the problem, and with the help of Anekāntavāda, he was able to argue for a position which can be called as close to "compatibilism" against absolute reliance on fate, as well as on perseverance, he argues:

> If it is maintained that all attainment of desirable objects is due to fate, then the question arises how it somehow happens that perseverance creates (i.e. decisively influences) fate. And if it is replied that fate is always a creation of fate, it follows that a man should never attain liberation and that all of his endeavour should always prove futile. If it is maintained that all attainment of objects is due to perseverance, then the question arises how it sometimes happens that fate creates perseverance. And if it is replied that perseverance is always a creation of perseverance, it follows that the endeavour of all people should always prove a success.[9]

These arguments against absolute reliance on fate, on the one hand, and absolute reliance on perseverance, on the other, are one step towards articulating the Jain position. This neither proves that fatalism is false, nor it is the opposite; what it does prove is that absolute fatalism is false and so is absolute reliance on perseverance. So, the emphasis here is more on avoiding absolute

[9] *daivādevārthasiddhiśced daivaṁ pauruṣataḥ katham* ।
daivataścedanirmokṣaḥ pauruṣaṁ niṣphalaṁ bhavet ।।
pauruṣādeva siddhiścet pauruṣaṁ daivataḥ katham ।
pauruṣāccedamoghaṁ syāt sarvaprāṇiṣu pauruṣam ।। – *Āptamīmāṁsā* 88-89

non-relativistic positions. Against these two exclusive and absolute positions, Samantabhadra argues for the Jain position:

> The happy and unhappy circumstances available to one that involve no premeditation on one's part are said to be due to one's fate; (whereas) the happy and unhappy circumstances available to one that involves a pre-meditation on one's part are said to be due to one's perseverance.[10]

Buddhipūrvaka and *abuddhipūrvaka* (with premeditation and without premeditation respectively) hold the key to this entire debate. What it seems to convey is that it is completely subjective to call a particular event as occurring due to fate or due to perseverance. For instance, if a person intends or premeditates to have a glass of water and eventually gets one, Samantabhadra would like to call it as an act of perseverance; whereas, on the other hand, if a person does not premeditate upon having a glass of water and still ends up drinking a glass of water, it would be called as an act of fate. In a way, this solves the problem when one analyses an event by taking into consideration the criteria of "premeditation". The message is that one can always take care of what one can and cannot premeditate upon. To put it in other terms, in cases where one has premeditated for a particular act to happen at a given instance of time, it is compatible with the oft-quoted phrase – "could have acted otherwise" – supporting free will; whereas, on the other hand, cases wherein one did not premeditate, it can be referred as an event where one "could not have acted otherwise" – supporting determinism.

Moral Responsibility in Relation to Free Will and Determinism

The notion of free will also has many repercussions on the problem of moral responsibility; the central question being whether

---

[10] *abuddhi-pūrvāpekṣāyāmiṣṭāniṣṭaṁ svadaivataḥ* ।
buddhipūrvavyapekṣāyāmiṣṭāniṣṭaṁ svapauruṣāt ।। – *Āptamīmāṁsā* 91

individuals are ever morally responsible for their actions and, if so, in what sense. It is indeed difficult to hold someone morally responsible if the act was not free from any external constraints or if it was not voluntary and thus determinism is cited as an excuse for not being morally responsible. To give an example, suppose a man is often motivated to steal and in accordance with determinism, he always does steal when his efforts to do so are unobstructed. But, according to determinist theories, he could not have acted otherwise. It follows that he cannot help being whatever he is. And thus, it is difficult to hold that man is morally responsible for his act of stealing. Intention then seems to play a vital role, for it is quite possible that the man never intended to steal and, yet, due to some psychological or neurological disorders, he could not help himself from stealing. The man cannot be held morally responsible for the act then. We come across one aphorism in the sixth chapter of the *Tattvārthasūtra*, which talks about the variation in bondage caused due to intention:

> Influx is differentiated on the basis of intensity (acute or mild) of thought-activity, intentional or unintentional nature of action, the substratum and its peculiar potency.[11]

Intention, thus, plays a key role in determining whether the agent could be held morally responsible for any activity. Further, while discussing about the substratum related to kārmic bondage, it is *jīva* and *ajīva.*[12] What is worth noticing is that this intention has been extended to such levels that even an approval/praise of a thing which was done by someone else attracts kārmic bondage on the part of the one who had approved that activity.[13]

---

[11] *tīvramandajñātābhāvavīryā 'dhikaraṇaviśeṣebhyastadviśeṣaḥ* ।
– *Tattvārthasūtra* 6.7

[12] *adhikaraṇaṁ jīvājīvāḥ* । – Ibid. 6.8

[13] *ādyaṁ saṁrambhasamārambhārambhayoga kr□takāritānumata-kaṣāyaviśeṣaistristristristriścatu-ścaikaśaḥ* । – Ibid. 6.9

Moreover, when determinism is cited as a refuge from one's moral commitments and responsibilities, it is not applied in totality. So, in cases where the person just wants to escape and get away, determinism becomes true; whereas, on the other hand, when that same person wants to achieve something or is aspiring for a goal which he/she really wants to accomplish, determinism is nowhere near to the discussion. In one of the *śloka*s in Amṛtacandra's *Ātmakhyāti*, it is said:

> Those *jīva*s, who regard the alien substance as absolutely responsible for the evolution of passions, like attachment, are devoid of right faith and are blind witted, being so, they are incapable of crossing the river of delusion.[14]

What is surprising is that this verse and the quotations supporting determinism (as stated in the earlier section on metaphysical determinism) are from the pen of the same author albeit in different contexts. This certainly means that he wanted to maintain determinism and at the same time speak of *jīva* being morally responsible for his acts. This cannot be possible without the help of different standpoints.

There is causal determinism as far as the *karma* theory is concerned; there is theological determinism when we take into account the omniscience of God; and there is metaphysical determinism in terms of the Jain position on the changing aspect of reality, the modification of a substance. In a way, there is determinism everywhere. But, as Anekāntavāda would not allow us to take an absolute stand on this problem, there is scope for free will as well, albeit in a different sense – it cannot grant contingency to the future events. Some might object that this is relativism, which is not giving any certain answers and also not what they were looking for, to which one could argue that it is relativism, no

---

[14] *rāga janmaninimittatāmparadravyamevakalayanti ye tute* ।
uttarantina hi mohavāhinīṁśuddhabodhavidhurāndhabuddhayaḥ ।।
– *Samayasāra-Kalaśa/Ātmakhyāti* 221

doubt, but of a different kind. There is a hint of certainty in each and every relative truth. It is relative insofar as it does not seek to repudiate the other aspects of the reality; it is certain of the particular viewpoint.[15]

The argument given by Samantabhadra, which is based on subjective criteria, might not be as appealing as his other arguments in the text. One needs to closely examine Samantabhadra's other works like the *Svayambhū-Stotra*, *Stuti-Vidyā* and *Ratnakaraṇḍa Śrāvakācāra* to find a clue as to whether he has given any arguments from the objective point of view in support of either or both the positions. Nevertheless, it once again motivates mankind to reconsider the problem of free will and see whether it is a problem at all – a trend more common among philosophers in the last few decades. Samantabhadra's argument from the subjective point of view attempts to dissolve the problem rather than assume that there is a problem and try to solve it. It can be said that the Jain position is quite close to the widely held view of compatibilism, wherein free will is said to be compatible with determinism and that neither of them are absolutely true or false.

References

Ācārya Amr̥tacandra, 1964, *Samayasāra-Kalaśa/Ātmakhyāti*, tr. P. Siddhantshastri, Sonagarh: Shri Digamber Jain Svadhyay Mandir Trust.

Ācārya Malliṣeṇasūri, 1968, *Syādvāda Mañjarī* (*A Commentary on Ācārya Hemacandra's Anyayoga-vyavacchedikā*), tr. F. Thomas, Delhi: Motilal Banarsidass.

Ācārya Samantabhadra, 1999, *Āptamīmāṁsā*, tr. N.J. Shah, Ahmedabad: L.D. Institute of Indology.

Chakravarty, A. (ed.), 2008, *Ācārya Kundakunda Samayasāra*, New Delhi: Bharatiya Jnana Pith.

---

[15] It is not the subject matter of this paper to deal with Anekāntavāda in detail. However, Anekāntavāda is not absolute non-absolutism. There have to be certain truths without which the system would collapse (see *Āptamīmāṁsā* 108).

Divākara, S., 1939, *Sanmatitarka*, ed. D. Malavania, Bombay: Shri Jain Shwetambar Education Board.

Dixit, K.K. (tr.), 2000, *Tattvārthasūtra*, by Umāsvāti, Ahmedabad: L.D. Institute of Indology.

Jain, M., 1987, *Kramabaddha Paryāya of Hukam Chand Bharill*, Jaipur: Pandit Todarmal Smarak Trust.

O'Connor, T., 2002, January 7, *Free Will*, retrieved 14 December 2017, from *Stanford Encyclopedia of Philosophy*: https://plato.stanford.edu/entries/freewill/.

Sanghavi, S. (ed.), 2009, *Tattvārthasūtra*, by Umāsvāti, Varanasi: Parshwanath Vidyapeeth.

Singh, R., 1974, *Jaina Concept of Omniscience*, Ahmedabad: L.D. Institute of Indology.

Taylor, R., 2006, "Determinism: A Historical Survey", in *Encyclopedia of Philosophy*, ed. D.M. Brochert, second edn, vol. III, pp. 4-23, New York: Thomson Gale.

Thomas, F. (ed.), 2014, *The Pravacanasāra of Kundakunda Ācārya: Together with the Commentary, Tattva-dīpikā, by Amṛtacandra Sūri*, New York: Cambridge University Press.

Todarmal, 2005, *Mokshamarg Prakashak*, ed. J. Jain, Bombay: Shri Kund-Kund Kahan Digamber Jain Tirth Suraksha Trust.

10

नियतिवाद और कथंचित् नियति

राहुलकुमार सिंह

नियतिवाद के अनुसार नियति ही सभी कार्यों का कारण है। नियति के सम्बन्ध में यह सर्वसामान्य अवधारणा है कि जो भी भवितव्य है, होनहार है, वही नियति है। भारतीय समाज में नियतिवाद, जो कि भाग्यवाद के रूप में भी प्रतिष्ठित रहा है, का आज भी पर्याप्त प्रभाव देखा जाता है। इस मान्यता के अनुसार यह सम्पूर्ण विश्व एक ऐसी शक्ति अथवा नियम-व्यवस्था से नियमित है जिसका उल्लंघन या छेड़छाड़ मनुष्य के लिए अशक्य है। यह वह नियामिक शक्ति है जिसके अनुशासन से समाज विश्व अनुशासित है। आकस्मिक घटनाओं के कारण के रूप में इसकी स्वीकृति है। इसीलिए अनेकश: हम आकस्मिक अद्‌भुत घटनाओं के घटित होने पर उसके रहस्य को नहीं जान पाते कि इनके घटित होने का कारण क्या था। इस प्रकार यह नियति विश्व की संचालिका, नियामिका, प्रेरक शक्ति के रूप में मान्य है। आचार्य मैथिलिशरण गुप्त के खण्डकाव्य "पंचवटी" की कुछ पंक्तियाँ इसका अत्यन्त ही सुन्दर चित्र प्रस्तुत करती हैं –

> बन्द नहीं होते अब भी चलते हैं, नियति नहीं के कार्य-कलाप।
> पर कितने एकान्त भाव से कितने शान्त और चुपचाप।।

इस प्रकार हम पाते हैं कि नियतिवाद भारतीय जनमानस में पूर्णतया समाविष्ट है और मनुष्य के व्यावहारिक जीवन में अत्यन्त ही महत्त्वपूर्ण स्थान रखता है। भारतीय जनमानस अपनी सफलताओं पर भाग्य अथवा नियति की ही दुहाई देते हुए दिखाई देता है साथ ही घोर से घोर कष्ट को भी नियतिवश ही स्वीकार कर जीवित रह लेता है।

मंखलिपुत्र गोशालक की विचारधारा के रूप में प्रतिष्ठित यह सिद्धान्त भारतीय मनीषा में सर्वत्र ही दृष्टिगोचर होता है। उपनिषद्, पुराण, महाकाव्य, नाटक, आगम, त्रिपिटक आदि इसके महत्त्व को स्पष्ट करने वाले उद्धरणों से ओत-प्रोत हैं। *श्वेताश्वतरोपनिषद्* में जगत् की उत्पत्ति के कारणों की चर्चा के अन्तर्गत काल, स्वभाव, नियति आदि का खण्डन करते हुए कहा गया है –

कालः स्वभावोनियतिर्यदृच्छाभूतानि योनिःपुरुषः इति चिन्त्या।
संयोगा एषां न त्वात्मभावादात्माप्यनीशःसुखदुःखहेतोः ।।
– *श्वेताश्वतरोपनिषद्* 1.2

अर्थात् काल, स्वभाव, नियति, यदृच्छा, पञ्चमहाभूत, योनि व पुरुष – इनका संयोग सृष्टि का कारण है, मात्र आत्मभाव से यह सृष्टि निर्मित नहीं हुई है, क्योंकि सुख-दुःख के कारण आत्मा भी स्वयं की ईश नहीं है।

वाल्मीकि भी नियति की कारणता को दर्शाने हेतु बाली की मृत्यु के पश्चात् लक्ष्मण, सुग्रीव आदि की सांत्वना हेतु श्रीराम के मुख से कहलाते हैं –

नियतिः कारणं लोके नियतिः कर्मसाधनम्।
नियतिः सर्वभूतानांनियोगेष्विहकारणम्।।
– *रामायण*, किष्किन्धाकाण्ड, सर्ग 25, श्लोक 4

अर्थात् जगत् में नियति ही सबका कारण है, नियति समस्त कार्यों का साधन है, नियति ही समस्त प्राणियों को विभिन्न कर्मों में नियुक्त करने में कारण है।

महाभारत में भी वर्णित है कि –

यथा यथाऽस्यप्राप्तव्यं, प्राप्नोत्येवतथातथा।
भवितव्यं यथा यच्च, भवत्येवतथातथा।।
– शन्तिपर्व, अध्याय 226, श्लोक 10

अर्थात् पुरुष को जो वस्तु जिस प्रकार मिलने वाली होती है, वह उसी प्रकार मिल ही जाती है। जिसका जो भी भवितव्य होता है, वह वैसा ही होता है।

इस प्रकार हम पाते हैं कि नियतिवाद का अर्थ है – जो, जब, जिसके द्वारा, जिसका, जिस नियम से होने वाला है, वह उसी काल में, उसी के द्वारा, उसी रूप में, उसी नियम से होता है।

प्राचीन वैदिक, बौद्ध एवं जैन परम्पराओं के अध्ययन से ज्ञात होता है कि इनमें नियतिवाद की संक्षिप्त चर्चा तो है किन्तु इसको बहुत अधिक महत्त्व नहीं दिया गया

है। अध्ययन से हमें ज्ञात होता है कि इन परम्पराओं की मान्य धारणा रही है कि व्यक्ति का भाग्य, उसका सामाजिक स्तर, उसके सुख-दुःख सभी उसकी इच्छा पर निर्भर हैं। भारतीय कर्मसिद्धान्त का सामान्य अर्थ ही है कि व्यक्ति अपनी इच्छा की स्वतन्त्रता के अनुसार कार्य कर सकता है। व्यक्ति की वर्तमान परिस्थिति किसी अपरिवर्तनीय सिद्धान्त (एकान्त नियति का सिद्धान्त) से संचालित नहीं होती अपितु उसके स्वयं के कर्मों से संचालित होती है, चाहे वे वर्तमान के हों या पूर्वकृत। सम्यक् मार्ग को ढूँढ़कर और उसे अपनाकर वह अपने जीवन को सुधार सकता है। यहाँ तक कि मोक्ष भी प्राप्त कर सकता है।

विभिन्न जैन ग्रन्थों में विद्वानों द्वारा नियतिवाद के स्वरूप को उद्घाटित किया गया है और एकान्त नियति का निरसन करते हुए कथंचित् नियति का स्वरूप दिग्दर्शित किया गया है। इसके अन्तर्गत काल, स्वभाव, नियति, कर्म और पुरुषार्थ/पुरुषकार को समवेत रूप से जगत् की घटनाओं के कारण के रूप में स्वीकार किया जाता है।

अन्य जैन विद्वानों की ही भाँति आचार्य हरिभद्र ने भी अपने ग्रन्थों में नियतिवाद के स्वरूप को निरूपित करते हुए उसकी ऐकान्तिकता का निरसन किया है। प्रस्तुत शोधपत्र में शास्त्रवार्त्तासमुच्चय में वर्णित विचार ही विशेष विचारणीय हैं। पूर्वपक्ष के रूप में नियतिवादी के मन्तव्य को स्पष्ट करते हुए वे लिखते हैं –

नियतेनैव रूपेणसर्वेभावाभवन्ति यत्।
ततो नियतिजाह्येते, तत्स्वरूपानुवेधतः।।
– स्तबक 2, श्लोक 61

अर्थात् क्योंकि जगत् की सभी वस्तुएँ एक नियत रूप वाली होती हैं इसलिए उनका कारण नियति नामक तत्त्वविशेष को मानना चाहिए और वह इस आधार पर कि नियति का जो स्वरूप है (अर्थात् नियत रूप वाली होना) वह इन वस्तुओं में ओत-प्रोत है।

यहाँ पर आचार्य हरिभद्र वादी द्वारा वस्तु के साधारण धर्म के रूप में स्वीकृत नियति जन्यता को उद्घाटित करते हैं।

तदनन्तर आचार्य हरिभद्र नियतिवाद के स्वरूप के स्पष्टीकरण के सन्दर्भ में इसकी प्रमाण सिद्धता को स्पष्ट करते हुए लिखते हैं –

यद्यदैव यतो यावत्तदैवततस्तथा।
नियतंजायते, न्यायात्क एतांवाधितुं क्षमः।।
– वही, श्लोक 62

> अर्थात् जिस वस्तु को जिस समय, जिस कारण से तथा जिस परिणाम में उत्पन्न होना होता है, वह वस्तु उसी समय, उसी कारण से तथा उसी परिणाम में नियत रूप से उत्पन्न होती है।

ऐसी दशा में नियति के सिद्धान्त का युक्तिपूर्वक खण्डन कौन सा वादी कर सकता है। प्रस्तुत कारिका से जाना जा सकता है कि नियतिवादी अपने मत के समर्थन में इस वस्तु-स्थिति को आधार बना रहा है कि प्रत्येक कार्य किसी नियत कारण से नियत परिपाटी द्वारा नियत काल लेकर उत्पन्न होता है। वस्तुतः इस प्रकार रखा जाने पर नियतिवाद, कालवाद तथा स्वभाववाद का ही सम्मिश्रित रूप बन जाता है। इस सन्दर्भ में उत्तरकालीन बौद्ध तार्किकों को हम सचमुच कहते पाते हैं कि "प्रत्येक वस्तु देश नियत होती है, काल नियत होती है, स्वभाव नियत होती है।" इसी गाथा की टीका में आचार्य यशोविजय लिखते हैं कि -

> नियतरूप विशिष्ट कार्य की उत्पत्ति ही नियति की सत्ता में प्रमाण है, क्योंकि यदि नियत रूप से कार्य की उत्पत्ति का कोई नियामक नहीं होगा तो कार्य की नियतरूपता आकस्मिक हो जाएगी। अर्थात् किसी वस्तु का कोई नियत रूप सिद्ध न हो सकेगा।
>
> — *स्याद्वाद्वकल्पलता, शास्त्रवार्तासमुच्चय*, स्तबक 2, श्लोक 62 की टीका

आगे वे लिखते हैं कि स्थिति के अभाव में कार्य का सम्यक् निश्चय अशक्य है। वे कहते हैं कि हमें यह दृष्टिगत होता है कि अनुकूल नियति के बिना मूँग भी नहीं पकती भले ही स्वभाव आदि (सभी कारण सामग्री) उपस्थित क्यों न हों; सचमुच मूँग का यह पकना अनियत रूप से तो नहीं होता (*शास्त्रवार्तासमुच्चय*, स्तबक 2, श्लोक 63)। ध्यातव्य है कि यहाँ पर भी स्वभावादि को नकारा नहीं गया है। नियति के पक्ष में एक अन्य तर्क देते हुए आचार्य हरिभद्र लिखते हैं —

> अन्यथाऽनियतत्वेनसर्वाभावः (सर्वभावः) प्रसज्यते।
> अन्योन्यात्मकतापत्तेः क्रियावैफल्यमेव च।।
>
> — वही, श्लोक 64

> अर्थात् यदि जगत् की वस्तुएँ नियत स्वरूप वाली न हों तो अनियत रूप वाली होने के कारण जगत् की सभी वस्तुओं का अभाव ही सिद्ध होता है। (क्योंकि ये वस्तुएँ एक नियत रूप वाली होकर तथा एक नियत कारण सामग्री की सहायता से अस्तित्व में आती हैं।) दूसरे इस दशा में जगत् की सभी वस्तुएँ एक दूसरे के रूप वाली होने के कारण सभी प्रकार की क्रिया निष्फल सिद्ध होनी चाहिए।

यहाँ पर आचार्य यशोविजय द्वारा "सर्वभावः" पाठ स्वीकार है तब यह अर्थ होता है – यदि ऐसा न हो तो अनियत रूप वाली होने के कारण प्रत्येक वस्तु दूसरी सभी वस्तुओं के स्वभाव वाली हो जानी चाहिए, जबकि सभी वस्तुएँ एक-दूसरे के रूप वाली होने के कारण सभी प्रकार की क्रिया निष्फल सिद्ध होनी चाहिए। अर्थात् नियतिवाद को न मानने पर सर्वात्मकता की आपत्ति आ जाती है।

नियतिवाद के स्वरूप को प्रस्तुत करने के बाद आचार्य हरिभद्र अपने ग्रन्थ *शास्त्रवार्त्ता समुच्चय* में कर्मवादी के पक्ष को प्रस्तुत करते हुए कर्मवादी द्वारा किए गए एकान्त नियति के खण्डन को दर्शाते हैं। उनका कहना है कि नियतिवादी द्वारा जो नियति की एकरूपता बताई गई है वह अशक्य है। वे लिखते हैं –

> नियतेर्नियतात्मत्वान्नियतानां समानता।
> तथाऽनियतभावे च बलात् स्यात् तद्विचित्रता।।
>
> – वही, श्लोक 69

> अर्थात् यदि नियति एक ही रूप वाली है तो नियत (अर्थात् नियति से उत्पन्न) वस्तुएँ भी समान रूप वाली होनी चाहिए; और यदि नियति अनियत रूप वाली (अर्थात् परस्पर असमान वस्तुओं को जन्म दे सकने वाली) है तब प्रस्तुतवादी को यह मानने के लिए विवश होना पड़ेगा कि यह नियति अनेक रूप वाली है।

इस नियति की एकमात्र कारणता के खण्डन में आचार्य हरिभद्र अगला तर्क देते हैं कि नियति के सामान्य स्वरूप से अथवा उसके परिणामों से उसमें विचित्रता की सिद्धि के लिए नियति से अन्य कोई उसका भेदक मानना पड़ेगा। वे लिखते हैं –

> यदि नियति, स्वरूप इत्यादि की दृष्टि से (अर्थात् स्वरूप तथा अवस्थान्तर प्राप्ति दोनों ही दृष्टि से) केवल नियति है (अन्य कुछ नहीं) तो उसे अनेक रूप वाली मानना तब तक युक्तिसंगत प्रतीत नहीं होता जब तक इस अनेकता के कारणभूत किसी तत्त्वान्तर की सत्ता स्वीकार न की जाए। तार्किक मर्म की अविरोधी मान्यता तो यही है। उदाहरण के लिए एक रूप वाला जल आकाश से नीचे गिरने के बाद अनेक रूप वाला तब तक नहीं बनता जब तक वह ऊसर आदि अनेक प्रकार की भूमियों में सम्मिश्रित नहीं होता। – वही, श्लोक 70–71

अर्थात् आकाश से जो जल बरसता है, वह सब जगह समान होता है। इसमें जो वैविध्य आता है वह ऊसर और उपजाऊ आदि विभिन्न भूमियों के सम्पर्क से ही होता है।

यह सिद्धान्त कि "नियति ही सभी वस्तुओं की हेतु है" इसके विरोध में आचार्य हरिभद्र लिखते हैं –

तद्भिन्नभेदकत्वे च तत्र तस्या न कर्तृता।
तत्कर्तृत्वे च चित्रत्वं तद्वत्तस्याप्यसंगतम्।।
- वही, श्लोक 72

अर्थात् यदि नियति से अतिरिक्त किसी तत्त्व को जगत् की वस्तुओं की परस्पर भिन्नता का कारण माना जाए तो यह मानना होगा कि इस अतिरिक्त तत्त्व का कारण नियति नहीं और यदि इस अतिरिक्त तत्त्व का कारण नियति है तो जगत् की वस्तुओं की परस्पर विभिन्नता के लिए इस तत्त्व को उत्तरदायी मानना वैसा ही है जैसा कि नियति को उसके लिए उत्तरदायी मानना।

यदि वादी यह कहे कि नियति का स्वभाव ही है कि वह परस्पर विभिन्न वस्तुओं को जन्म देती है तो ऐसा कहने से स्वभाववाद का आश्रय लेने के कारण नियतिवाद का ही त्याग हो जाता है (वही, श्लोक 73)।

इस प्रकार आचार्य हरिभद्र नियति की ऐकान्तिकता के खण्डन के साथ-साथ काल, स्वभाव, कर्म इत्यादि की ऐकान्तिकता का खण्डन करते हैं और निष्कर्ष स्वरूप कहते हैं –

अतः कालादयः सर्वे, समुदायेनकारणम्।
गर्भादेः कार्यजातस्य, विज्ञेयान्यायवादिभिः।।
- वही, श्लोक 79

अर्थात् तार्किक मार्ग का अनुसरण करने वाले को मानना चाहिए कि काल आदि सब तत्त्व (अर्थात् काल, स्वभाव, नियति, कर्म) आपस में मिलकर ही गर्भप्रवेश आदि कार्यों के कारण बनते हैं।

इस प्रकार प्रस्तुत कारिका के आधार पर हम यह कह सकते हैं कि कालवाद, स्वभाववाद तथा नियतिवाद के विरुद्ध उठाई गई कर्मवादी की आपत्तियों से हरिभद्र स्वयं तत्त्वतः सहमत हैं। उनका नया सुझाव इतना ही है कि काल, स्वभाव, नियति तथा कर्म चारों ही मिलकर जगत् की घटनाओं के कारण बनते हैं। वस्तुतः कालवाद, स्वभाववाद और नियतिवाद के बीच पारस्परिक मतभेद इतने गहरे नहीं हैं जितने गहरे मतभेद इन तीनों और कर्मवाद के मध्य हैं। यदि प्रथम तीन वादों को कार्य-कारणवाद यह सामान्य नाम दिया जाए तो कहना होगा कि हरिभद्र का अपना मत कार्य-कारणवाद तथा कर्मवाद के मध्य समन्वय स्थापित करने का है। इसलिए वे पुनः कहते भी हैं –

न चैकैकत एवेह क्वचित् किश्चिदपीक्ष्यते।
तस्मात् सर्वस्य कार्यस्य सामग्री जनिका मता।
- वही, श्लोक 80

> अर्थात् उक्त तत्त्व अकेले-अकेले कहीं भी तथा किसी भी कार्य को जन्म देते नहीं पाए जाते, अतः यही माना जाना चाहिए कि ये तत्त्व सभी कार्यों का कारण सम्मिलित रूप से बनते हैं।

इस प्रकार हम देखते हैं कि आचार्य हरिभद्र द्वारा एकान्त नियति के स्थान पर कथंचित् नियति को स्वीकार किया गया है। साथ ही जैनदर्शन में काललब्धि और सर्वज्ञता ऐसे प्रत्यय हैं जिनके माध्यम से भी कथंचित् नियति का प्रवेश हो जाता है। जब हम सूक्ष्म दृष्टि से अवलोकन करते हैं तो पाते हैं कि जैनदर्शन में कथंचित् नियति का स्वीकरण होते हुए भी काललब्धि और सर्वज्ञता को एकान्त नियति से पृथक् सिद्ध किया गया है; क्योंकि जैनदर्शन में नियति को कारण मानते हुए भी उसमें काल, स्वभाव आदि अन्य कारणों को भी स्थान दिया गया है। जैनदर्शन की यह मान्यता है कि अनादिकालीन मिथ्या दृष्टि जीव काललब्धि आने पर ही सम्यक्त्व और मोक्ष की प्राप्ति करता है। काललब्धि से आशय है समुचित काल की प्राप्ति। उसका होना नियत होता है तभी काललब्धि होती है। ध्यातव्य है कि काललब्धि की अवधारणा "कालवाद" से पृथक् है। कालवाद में स्वीकृत काल की एकान्तिक कारणता के विपरीत काललब्धि में काल की कारणता के साथ ही कर्मपुरुषार्थ आदि की कारणता भी स्वीकार की गई है। जो कि नियति या काल की कथंचित् कारणता का ही मार्ग प्रशस्त करती है।

इसी तरह सर्वज्ञता के प्रत्यय को लें तो जैनदर्शन में सर्वज्ञ शब्द का प्रयोग केवल ज्ञानी के लिए किया जाता है। केवल ज्ञानी समस्त द्रव्यों और उसके पर्यायों को साक्षात् देखता एवं जानता है। यह सर्वज्ञ की सामान्य अवधारणा है और इस अर्थ में नियतिवाद का प्रवेश निश्चित हो जाता है। सर्वज्ञत्व के इस अर्थ को लेकर कि "सर्वज्ञ हस्तामलकवत् सभी जागतिक पदार्थों की त्रैकालिक पर्यायों को जानता है", जैन विद्वानों में काफी ऊहापोह किया है। कुछ विद्वानों ने सर्वज्ञता का अर्थ आत्मज्ञता किया है। इस अर्थ में हम इसमें एकान्त नियति के प्रवेश से बच जाते हैं। आचार्य हरिभद्र तो अपने तर्क ग्रन्थों में त्रैकालिक सर्वज्ञता का हेतुवाद से समर्थन कर चुके थे किन्तु जब उनको उस हेतुवाद में त्रुटि व विरोध दिखाई दिया तब उन्होंने सर्वज्ञत्व का अर्थ किया – सर्वसम्प्रदाय अविरुद्ध (*दर्शन और चिन्तन*, पृ० 553, उद्धृत, *जैनदर्शन में कारण-कार्यव्यवस्था : एक समन्वयात्मक दृष्टिकोण*, पृ० 301)।

त्रिकालज्ञ-सर्वज्ञता की यह समस्या है कि यदि सर्वज्ञ त्रिकालज्ञ है तो फिर वह भविष्य को भी जानेगा, लेकिन अनियत भविष्य को तो जाना नहीं जा सकता। यहाँ यह ध्यातव्य है कि सर्वज्ञ के जानने मात्र से दूसरे का पुरुषार्थ प्रभावित नहीं

होता। जैसा होता है उसे वे वैसा जानते हैं। इस अर्थ में नियतिवाद नहीं आता। परन्तु उन्होंने जैसा जाना है वैसा ही होगा, इस पक्ष को मानने पर नियतिवाद की आशंका आती है। इसको समझने के लिए आगम का एक उदाहरण प्रस्तुत है –

> प्रसन्नचन्द्र राजर्षि मुनि बनकर नगर के बाहर ध्यानस्थ थे। उस समय वहाँ एक राजा का आक्रमण हो गया। उनके कानों में आक्रमण की बात पहुँची तो उनका राजत्व जाग उठा और वे प्रतिहिंसा और प्रतिकार की भावना में बहने लगे। उस समय भगवान् महावीर से राजा श्रेणिक ने प्रश्न किया कि यदि प्रसन्नचन्द्र राजर्षि इस समय काल करें तो कहाँ उत्पन्न होंगे। भगवान् ने उत्तर दिया कि वे इस समय काल करें तो सातवीं नरक में उत्पन्न होंगे। थोड़ी देर पश्चात् ही मुनि प्रसन्नचन्द्र ने अपना मुकुट संभालने के लिए सिर पर हाथ रखा तो उन्हें ज्ञात हुआ कि वे तो मुनि हैं और मुनि बन गए हैं। युद्ध की भावना उसके लिए उचित नहीं है। भावधारा एकदम बदल जाती है। संक्लेश के स्थान पर विशुद्धि के भावों का आरोहण होता है। अब वे बाह्य के बजाय अन्तर में विद्यमान कषाय-रूपी शत्रुओं से युद्ध करने लगे और उनकी निर्मलता बढ़ने लगी। उस समय राजा श्रेणिक ने भगवान् से पुनः वही प्रश्न किया तो भगवान् ने उत्तर दिया कि उसे केवल ज्ञान हो गया है। – वही, पृ० 300

यह उदाहरण इस बात को सिद्ध करता है कि व्यक्ति अपना पुरुषार्थ करने को स्वतन्त्र है तथा जो केवली होता है उसे जानता है। सर्वज्ञता का यह स्वरूप स्वीकार किया जाए तो नियतिवाद का प्रवेश नहीं होता। *भगवतीसूत्र* भी व्यक्ति के किए हुए समस्त कर्मों और उसके फल को नियति के अधीन नहीं मानता बल्कि स्वीकृत मानता है। यहाँ उत्थान, बल, पुरुषार्थ को मान्य किया गया है। जैनदर्शन के अनुसार निकाचित और अनिकाचित के रूप में कर्मों के दो भेद हैं। निकाचित कर्म प्रगाढ़ बन्धमय होते हैं। उनका फल भोगना ही पड़ता है। बिना भोगे निर्धारण नहीं होता। अनिकाचित को तपस्या द्वारा क्षीण किया जा सकता है। अतः न एकान्त-नियतिवाद ही स्वीकार है और न अनियतवाद ही।

संकल्प की स्वतन्त्रता और एकान्त-नियतिवाद की व्याधकता पर समस्त भारतीय दार्शनिक अपने-अपने ढंग से विचार करते हैं और अधिकांश उत्तर देते हैं कि मनुष्य अपने सामर्थ्य से मोक्ष अथवा पूर्णता की स्थिति को प्राप्त कर सकता है। फलस्वरूप इस चिन्तना में नियतिवाद का घोर विरोध हुआ है। लेकिन यह बात उतनी ही सत्य है कि भारतीय व्यावहारिक जीवन में नियतिवाद किसी न किसी रूप में प्रतिष्ठित रहा है। माघ के शब्दो में –

> विद्वान् न तो केवल दैव का सहारा लेते हैं और न तो केवल पौरुष पर ही स्थित रहते हैं। जिस प्रकार सत् कवि शब्द और अर्थ दोनों का आश्रय ग्रहण करता है, उसी प्रकार विद्वान् भी दैव और पुरुष दोनों को जीवन में आवश्यक समझता है (शिशुपालवध 2.86)।

अन्ततः हम यह कह सकते है कि जैनदर्शन नियतिवाद को पूर्णतः अस्वीकार नहीं करता वरन् उसे कथंचित् स्वीकार करता है। राधाकृष्णन के शब्दों में – यद्यपि आत्मापूर्व निर्धारित घटनाओं (नियति) के बन्धन से सर्वथामुक्त नहीं है तो भी वह अतीत को कुछ हद तक पराभूत कर नए पथ की ओर प्रवृत्त और निर्देशित कर सकती है। मनुष्य अपनी स्वतन्त्रता से अनिवार्य (नियति) को अपने लिए उपयोगी बना लेता है। इसी अर्थ में मानव को स्वतन्त्र कर्त्ता माना गया है। व्यक्ति की इस स्वतन्त्र इच्छाशक्ति के नियोजन के बदले मात्र भाग्य के प्रवाह में अपने आप को बहा देना निष्क्रियता अथवा पंगुता की निशानी है, जो कतई अपेक्षित नहीं है। जीवन को सक्रिय, प्राणवान एवं कर्त्तव्यनिष्ठ बनाने के लिए महावीर द्वारा प्रतिपादित नियति एवं पुरुषार्थ का समन्वित दर्शन ही उपादेय है।

सन्दर्भ

आचार्य हरिभद्र, 2002, *शास्त्रवार्तासमुच्चय*, अनु० कृष्ण कुमार दीक्षित, लालभाई दलपतभाई भारतीय संस्कृतिविद्यामन्दिर, अहमदाबाद।

जैन, श्वेता, 2008, *जैनदर्शन में कारण-कार्य व्यवस्था : एक समन्वयात्मक दृष्टिकोण*, पार्श्वनाथ विद्यापीठ वाराणसी और प्राच्य विद्यापीठ, शाजापुर।

महाभारत (पचम खण्ड), शान्तिपर्व, अनु० रामनारायणदत्त शास्त्री, गीताप्रेस, गोरखपुर, 2013।

श्वेताश्वतरोपनिषद्, अनु० महेशानन्दगिरी, श्रीदक्षिणामूर्ति मठ प्रकाशन, वाराणसी, 1976।

शास्त्रवार्त्तासमुच्चय और उसकी व्याख्या - स्याद्वादकल्पलता का हिन्दी विवेचन (स्तबक 2), अनु० बदरीनाथ शुक्ल, दिव्यदर्शन ट्रस्ट, मुम्बई, 1979।

शिशुपालवध महाकाव्यम्, अनु० रामप्रताप त्रिपाठी, भारतीय विद्यासंस्थान, वाराणसी, 2010।

श्रीमद्वाल्मीकीय रामायण (भाग 1), अनु० जानकीनाथ शर्मा, गीताप्रेस, गोरखपुर, 2012।

Group photo of delegates after valedictory function

Summary of Presentations in Seminar

Shrinetra Pandey

INTERNATIONAL School for Jain Studies, New Delhi organized a two-day International Seminar on "Determinism in Śramaṇika Traditions (Particularly Jainism and Buddhism): Their Moral and Ethical Effects" in association with Mangalayatan University, Aligarh on 11-12 January 2018. The inaugural function held on 11 January 2018. Pt. Hukum Chand Bharill, a renowned scholar of Jainism, was the chief guest and Dr Shugan Chand Jain, Chairman, International School for Jain Studies, New Delhi delivered the keynote address. The inaugural session was chaired by Professor (Brig.) P.S. Siwach, Hon. Vice-Chancellor, Mangalayatan University, Aligarh. Welcome address and theme of the seminar was presented by Dr Shrinetra Pandey, Joint Director, International School for Jain Studies, New Delhi and vote of thanks was by Professor J.L. Jain, Dean, Humanities, Mangalayatan University, Aligarh.

Dr Bharill argued that every substance of the world has attributes of permanence, origination and destruction. New mode is produced and present mode is destructed in each substance at every moment simultaneously and at the same time while the substance retains its existence. Thus, every substance changes in a certain defined order known as *kramabaddha-paryāya* (serial existence of modes).

Dr Shugan C. Jain presented the basic tenets of Jainism keeping in mind the main traits of Jains indicated by their being varyingly referred as *śramaṇas* (believers in self effort to achieve their objective of self-reliance), *vrātyas* (one who observes vows, fasts) and *niggantha* (without any possessions) in Indian philosophical literature. They believe in the eternal existence of individual soul in each living being. This mundane soul is capable of attaining its pure soul state/*mokṣa* through its own self-effort. He argued that the status of a mundane soul at any time instant in future seems to be governed by a number of factors making its prediction probabilistic and not adhering to the doctrine of Niyativāda. On the other hand, in the case of pure soul, being in a state of infinite knowledge and bliss and not affected by external beings is predicable exactly and hence supports Niyativāda. He discussed these concepts vis-à-vis *niścaya*, *vyavahāra naya*, ethics, *karma* doctrine and story literature.

After the inaugural session, seven technical sessions were organized in these two days (11-12 January 2018). List summarizing the speakers with their paper topics is given below:

Thursday, 11 January 2018		
Session I: Chaired by Professor P.C. Kanthaliya (Udaipur)		
Sl. No.	*Name of the Speaker*	*Topic*
Paper 1	Prof. M.K. Bhandari (Hyderabad)	Niyativāda (Fatalism) vs Karma-vāda: Are They Contradictory or Complimentary? Holistic Perspective from the Prism of Jainism
Paper 2	Professor Ashok K. Singh (Delhi)	Divinity in the Mahābhārata
Paper 3	Br. Sumat Prakash Ji	Nature of Determinism in Jainism (Jain Darśana meiṅ Niyativāda kā Svarūpa)
Paper 4	Dr Meenal Katarnikar (Mumbai)	Determinism in the Śramaṇa Ethics: Its Interrogation in the Contemporary Context
Paper 5	Dr. Kamini Gogri (Mumbai)	Free Will in the Realm of Morality: Examining Jain

Session II: Chaired by Professor S.L. Godawat (Udaipur)

Sl. No.	*Name of the Speaker*	*Topic*
Paper 6	Shri Saket Jain* (Singapore)	Impact of Niyativāda on Behaviour, Ethics and Morality
Paper 7	Ms Varsha Shah (Mumbai)	Philosophical Views of Heretics Depicted in Lotus Pool (Essence of Pauṇḍarīkakamala in Puṣkarṇī Lake) of Sūtra
Paper 8	Shri Nayan Jain* (Singapore)	The Primary Focus of Niyativāda in Jain Philosophy: Kartāvāda vs Akartāvāda
Paper 9	Dr Sandeep Shandilya (Aligarh)	Karma vs Niyativāda: A Philosophical Discourse Based on the Concept of Oneness of Śūnya (Zero) and Ananta (Infinity)
Paper 10	Shri Himanshu Jain* (USA)	What Role Do I Play in Shaping My Future?: A Jain Perspective on Determinism

Session III: Chaired by Dr Meenal Katarnikar (Mumbai)

Paper 11	Smt. Chhaya Seth (Bengaluru)	Karma Doctrine vis-à-vis Niyativāda
Paper 12	Shri Atmarpit Devang (Dharampur)	Niyativāda vis-à-vis Doctrine of Karma
Paper 13	Shri Jinesh R. Seth (Mumbai)	Determinism, Free Will and Morality: A Jain Perspective
Paper 14	Ms Sangeeta Shah (Mumbai)	Karma Doctrine and Niyativāda
Paper 15	Shri Sayyam Jain (Jaipur)	Place of Determinism in Five Co-Factors

cont.

Thursday, 12 January 2018		
Session IV: Chaired by Professor M.K. Bhandari (Hyderabad)		
Sl. No.	*Name of the Speaker*	*Topic*
Paper 16	Dr Surendra Singh Pokharna (Ahmedabad)	Concept of Niyativāda or "Determinism" and Indeterminism in Science and Jainism
Paper 17	Professor P.C. Kanthalia (Udaipur)	Determinism and the Karma Theory of Jainism
Paper 18	Professor Christopher K. Chapple* (USA)	Nature of Determinism in Jainism (Jain Darśana meiṁ Niyativāda kā Svarūpa)
Paper 19	Professor S.L. Godawat (Udaipur)	Will: An Exercise in Comparative Theology
Session V: Chaired by Professor Ashok K. Singh (Delhi)		
Paper 20	Br. Hema Chand Jain 'Hem' (Bhopal)	Omniscience and Niyativāda
Paper 21	Dr Anupam Jash (Durgapur)	Free Will and Niyativāda of Gośāla: An Appraisal
Paper 22	Dr Navin Kumar Srivastav (Pune)	The Concept of "Niyativāda" as Depicted in Jainism
Paper 23	Dr Swarnalata Jain (Udaipur)	Advantage and Disadvantage of Niyativāda and Puruṣārthavāda (Niyativāda aur Puruṣārthavāda se Lābha-Hāni)
Session VI: Chaired by Br Hema Chand Jain 'Hem' (Bhopal)		

Sl. No.	*Name of the Speaker*	*Topic*
Paper 24	Dr Rahul Kumar Singh (Pratapgarh)	नियतिवाद एवं कथंचित् नियति
Paper 25	Dr Rakesh Jain (Nagpur)	कार्योत्पत्ति में नियति : मात्र ज्ञापक, कारक नहीं
Paper 26	Dr Vedbyas Pandey (Varanasi)	नियतिवाद "पुब्बकम्मपिलोतिकबुद्धअपदान" के परिप्रेक्ष्य में
Paper 27	Pt Yogesh Shastri	जैन धर्म में नियतिवाद
Paper 28	Pt Hemant Gandhi	नियतिवाद : जैन कर्म सिद्धान्त के परिप्रेक्ष्य में

**The overseas scholars presented their papers via SKYPE.*

Besides the above well researched papers presented, we received papers from the following scholars:

1. "Concept of 'Free Will' in Early Buddhism" by Professor Bimalendra Kumar (Dept. of Pali & Buddhist Studies, BHU, Varanasi).
2. "Krama-Baddha-Paryāya: A Scientific Analysis" by Professor N.L. Kachhara (Former Principal, Motilal Nehru Regional Engineering College, Allahabad).
3. "Concept of Determinism and Indeterminism in Science and Jainism" by Dr Ratnakumar S. Shah (Pune).
4. "Determinism in Jain Dharma" by Er Manmohan Chandra Jain (Korb, CG).
5. "Jain and Buddhist Doctrines Support both Niyativada and Karma" by Dr Siddharth Jain (IIMT University, Meerut).
6. "Ethics in 21st Century: Jainism Perspectives" by Dr Monika Mehrotra (IIMT University, Meerut).

Due to lack of the time and absence of some of these speakers, these research papers could not be presented but were informally discussed.

At the end of the session Professor J.L. Jain, Dean, Humanities, Mangalayatan University, Aligarh presented the report of the seminar; Professor (Brig.) P.S. Siwach, Vice-Chancellor, Mangala-yatan University gave the vote of thanks.

All the scholars and distinguished gathering who attended the seminar appreciated the in-depth discussions and thoughtful research presentation in the seminar and discussions.

About Organizing Institutions

Mangalayatan University (MU) (www.mangalayatan.in) is promoted by Acharya Kundkund Educational Society and Shri Pawan Jain, an eminent journalist, industrialist, philanthropist and dedicated to the cause of education. It has been established under "The Mangalayatan University, Uttar Pradesh Act, 2006" and notification issued on 30 October 2006, with the right to provide higher education and authorized to award degrees specified in UGC Act. The university is also a member of Association of Indian Universities (AIU). Programmes offered by the university have regulatory approval by authorities like UGC, National Council for Teacher Education (NCTE), Bar Council of India (BCI), Pharmacy Council of India (PCI) and Council of Architecture (CoA).

The university offers higher education in the disciplines of Engineering, Biotechnology, Pharmacy, Business Management, Journalism and Mass Communication, Computer Application, Hospitality Management, Education and Research, Visual & Performing Art and Jain Philosophy. The faculty at MU consists of several highly qualified and motivated individuals from the IITs, NITs, foreign universities and other high-quality institutions. MU's vision is to give students from all kinds of backgrounds a quality educational experience leading to legitimately rewarding career opportunities.

It is ensured that the students acquire a strong sense of community responsibility, thanks to the environment they live in, symbolized best by the grand Jain Temple on the campus. With campus residents, the 72-acre lush green campus of MU sports a vibrant, energetic feel at all times. Some student initiatives like *Kadam* and *Parivartan* do stellar works in the nearby village areas in the fields of education, hygiene, health and environmental awareness. The vision is to develop a spirit of inquisitive questioning, an ability to excel in the pressure of a fast-changing professional world and a desire to grow into a personality than a person, in an environment that fosters strong moral and ethical values, teamwork, community service and environmental consciousness.

International School for Jain Studies (ISJS) (www.isjs.in) is a leading institution for academic studies of Jainism was set up in 2005. Its mission is to introduce academic studies of Jainism in the universities globally. So far 764 person from 279 universities/schools/institutes of thirty-five countries, primarily from the US, have attended our summer and winter programmes. ISJS also conducts seminars, undertakes funded research projects and publishes papers and books on various aspects of Jainism and its application and relevance in today's society. ISJS is associated with a number of universities and research organizations and leading scholars of Jainism globally. Now, ISJS has merged its operations with the prestigious Amar Prerana Trust (APT) of Pune for enhancing its resources.

The main objective of ISJS is to support a comprehensive, scholarly and experimental introduction of Jain academic studies in the universities around the world in general and North America in particular. Therefore, ISJS implements its programmes by a process of careful screening of potential participants and faculty, well-researched curriculum, engaging participants in intensive academic studies, living in Jain hostels, enjoy Jain food, providing interactions with Jain laity and monks, observe and participate in rituals and pilgrimage to make it a lived Jain experience.

Consolidated Bibliography

Ācārya Amṛtacandra, 1964, *Samayasāra-Kalaśa/Ātmakhyāti*, tr. P. Siddhantshastri, Sonagarh: Shri Digamber Jain Svadhyay Mandir Trust.

——, 1970, *Tattvārthasāra*, Varanasi: Shri Ganeshprasad Varni Granthamala.

Ācārya Haribhadra, 1932, *Viṁśati-Viṁśikā*, ed. K.V. Abhyankar, Pune: Aryabhushan Mudranalay.

Ācārya Kundakunda, 2012, *Samayasāra*, ed. V.K. Jain, Dehradun: Vikalp Printers.

Ācārya Malliṣeṇasūri, 1968, *Syādvāda Mañjarī (A Commentary on Ācārya Hemacandra's Anyayoga-vyavacchedikā)*, tr. F. Thomas, Delhi: Motilal Banarsidass.

Ācārya Nanesh, 2008, *Jin Dhammo*, Bikaner: Akhil Bhartiya Sadhumargi Jain Shravak Sangh.

Ācārya Nemicandra, 1999, *Gommaṭasāra-Karmakāṇḍa*, ed. A.N. Shastri, New Delhi: Bharatiya Jnanapith.

——, 2000, *Gommaṭasāra-Jīvakāṇḍa*, ed. A.N. Shastri, New Delhi: Bharatiya Jnana Pith.

——, 2004, *Gommaṭasāra-Jīvakāṇḍa*, vol. I, ed. A.N. Shastri, New Delhi: Bharatiya Jnana Pith.

——, 2010, *Dravyasaṅgraha*, tr. N. Balbir, Mumbai: Hindi Granth Karyalaya.

Ācārya Pūjyapāda, 1997, *Sarvārthasiddhi*, ed. P. Shastri, New Delhi: Bharatiya Jnana Pith.

Ācārya Samantabhadra, 1999, *Āptamīmāṁsā*, tr. N.J. Shah, Ahmedabad: L.D. Institute of Indology.

——, 2016, *Āptamimāṁsā*, tr. V.K. Jain, Dehradun: Vikalp Printers.

Aṅguttara Nikāyo, vol. 1, Igatpuri: Vipassana Research Institute, 1998.

Animal Kill Counter, n.d., retrieved 18 August 2018, from Occupy for Animals: http://occupyforanimals.weebly.com/animal-kill-counter.html.

Babb, L., 1996, *Absent Lord: Ascetics and Kings in a Jain Ritual Culture*, Berkeley, CA: University of California Press.

Barua, B.M., 1920, *The Ajivikas*, Calcutta: University of Calcutta.

Basham, A.L., 2002, *History and Doctrines of the Ājīvikas: A Vanished Indian Religion*, Delhi: Motilal Banarsidass.

Bhandari, N. and S.S. Pokharna, 2017, "Syadavada and Anekantvada in the Modern Scientific Context", in *Compendium on Science and Mathematics in* Jainism, Ladnun, Rajasthan: Bhagawan Mahavir International Research Center for Scientific Research and Innovative Studies in Social Sciences.

Bhandari, N., 2015, *Jainism: The Eternal and Universal Path to Enlightenment*, Jaipur: Prakrit Bharti Academy.

Bhattacharya, R., 2011, *Studies on the Cārvāka/Lokāyata*, London: Anthem Press.

Bhargava, D.N., 1968, *Jain Ethics*, Delhi: Motilal Banarsidass.

Blackburn, S., n.d., *Review of Thomas Nagel, The Last Word*, retrieved 30 January 2018, from Faculty of Philosophy: http://www2.phil.cam.ac.uk/~swb24/reviews/Nagel.htm.

Bohm, D., 1980, *Wholeness and the Implicate Order*, London: Routledge & Kegan Paul.

Bowker, J., 1997, *Oxford Dictionary of World Religions*, Oxford: Oxford University Press.

Buchanan, M., 2011, "Quantum Minds: Why We Think like Quarks", *New Scientist*, 211(2828): 34-37.

Chakravarty, A. (ed.), 2008, *Ācārya Kundakunda's Samayasāra*, New Delhi: Bharatiya Jnanapith.

Chapple, C.K. (ed.), 2003, *Reconciling Yogas: Haribhadra's Collection of Views on Yoga – with a New Translation of Haribhadra's Yogadṛṣṭisamuccaya*, tr. C.K. Chapple and J.T. Casey, Albany, NY: State University of New York Press.

Cullavagga, Igatpuri: Vipassana Research Institute, 1998.

Dīgha Nikāya vol. II, Igatpuri: Vipassana Research Institute, 1993.

Divākara, S., 1939, *Sanmatitarka*, ed. D. Malvania, Bombay: Shri Jain Shwetambar Education Board.

Dixit, K.K., 2002, *Śāstra-vārtā-samuccaya of Haribhadra Sūri,* Ahmedabad: L.D. Institute of Indology.

Doniger, W., 2014, *On Hinduism*, Oxford: Oxford University Press.

Doshi, R.L., 1977, *Tīrthaṅkara Caritra*, vol. III, Sailana: Akhila Bhāratīya Sādhu Mārgī Jain Saṁskṛti Saṅgha.

——, "Free Will and Voluntarism in Jainism", 2014, in *Free Will, Agency, and Selfhood in Indian Philosophy*, ed. M.R. Bryant, pp. 68-84, New York: Oxford University Press.

Goldsmith, E., 1990, "Evolution, Neo-Darwinism and the Paradigm of Science", *The Ecologist*, 20(2): 67-73.

Gupta, C. (ed.), 1968, *Dhammapada,* Varanasi: Chaukhambha Vidyabhavan.

How Many Species We Are Losing? (15 December 2018), retrieved 12 August 2019, from WWF: https://wwf.panda.org/-discover/our_focus/biodiversity/biodiversity/

Jain, J. L., 2018, *Essence of Samaysar,* Chennai: Dept. of Jainology, University of Madras.

——, 2020, *Essence of Pravacansāra*, ed. P. Jain, Chennai: Dept. of Jainology, University of Madras.

Jain, M., 1987, *Kramabaddha Paryāya of Hukam Chand Bharill,* Jaipur: Pandit Todarmal Smarak Trust.

Jain, S.C. (ed.), 2011, *Jainism: Key to Reality* (*Tattvārthasūtra by Āc. Umā Swāmi*), Hastinapur: Digambar Jain Trilok Shodh Sansthan.

——, 2018, *Jainism* (*For Young Inquisitive*), Delhi: International School for Jain Studies.

Jaina Sūtras (*The Acarangasūtra, The Kaplasūtra*), vol. I, tr., H. Jacobi, Delhi: Low Price Publications, 1968.

Jaini, P.S., 1998, *The Jaina Path of Purification*, Delhi: Motital Banarsidass.

Jayatilleke, K.N., 1963, *Early Buddhist Theory of Knowledge*, London: George Allen and Unwin Ltd.

———, 1972, *Ethics in Buddhist Perspective*, Kandy, Sri Lanka: Buddhist Publication Society.

Jnanamati, G., 2007, *Jain Bharati: The Essence of Jainism*, Hastinapur: Digambar Jain Institute of Cosmographic Research.

Johnson, W.J., 1995, *Harmless Souls: Karmic Bondage and Religious Change in Early Jainism with Special Reference to Umāsvāti and Kundakunda*, Delhi: Motilal Banarsidass.

Kachhara, N.L., 2014, *Scientific Explorations of Jain Doctrine*, parts 1 & 2, Delhi: Motilal Banarsidass.

Kachhara, N.L., S.R. Tater and Samani U. Pragya, 2017, "Karma, Living Systems, Genes and Human Performance", in *Scientific Perspectives of Jainism*, ed. Samani C. Prajna, N.L. Kachhara and N. Bhandari, pp. 115-49, Ladnun, Rajasthan: Bhagwan Mahaveer International Center for Scientific Research and Social Innovation Studies.

Kalghati, T.G., 1969, *Jain View of Life*, Solapur: Jain Sanskriti Sanrakshak Sangh.

Kelting, W., 2001, *Singing to the Jinas: Jain Laywomen, Mandal Singing, and the Negotiations of Jain Devotion*, New York: Oxford University Press.

———, 2009, *Heroic Wives: Rituals, Stories and the Virtues of Jain Wifehood*, New York: Oxford University Press.

Knapton, S., 2014, "Half of World's Animals Have Disappeared since 1970", *The Telegraph*, 30 September, retrieved 30 July 2018, from https://www.telegraph.co.uk/news/earth/wildlife/-11129163/Half-of-worlds-animals-have-disappeared-since-1970.html.

Kothari, D., 1985, "The Complementarity Principle and Eastern Philosophy", In *Neils Bohr: A Centenary Volume*, ed. A.P. Kennedy, pp. 325-31, Cambridge, MA: Harvard University Press.

Madhukar Muni (ed.), 1989, *Ācārāṅgasūtra*, vol. I, Beawar: Shri Agam Prakashan Samiti.

—— (ed.), 2003, *Vyākhyāprajñpti* (*Bhagavatīsūtra*, vol. III, Beawar: Shri Agam Prakashan Samiti.

—— (ed.), 2006, *Upāsaka-daśāṅgasūtra*, Beawar: Shri Agam Prakashan Samiti.

Majjhima Nikāya, vols I, II & V, Igatpuri: Vipassana Research Institute, 1955.

Malalasekera, G. (ed.), 1990, *Encyclopedia of Buddhism*, Ceylon: Buddhist Council of Ceylon, Ministry of Cultural Affairs, Government of Sri Lanka.

Mehta, M.L., 1998, *Jain Philosophy: An Introduction*, Bangalore: Bharatiya Vidya Bhavan.

Monier-Williams, M., 1899, *A Sanskrit-English Dictionary*, Oxford: Clarendon Press.

Nahar, P.C. and K.C. Ghosh, 1917, *An Epitome of Jainism: Being a Critical Study of Its Metaphysics, Ethics, and History, etc. in Relation to Modern Thought*, Calcutta: H. Dubey Publication.

Neppe, V.M. and E.R. Close, 2012, *Reality Begins with Consciousness: A Paradigm Shift That Works*, Washington: Brain Voyage.

Neils, Bohr, 1985, *A Centenary Volume*, ed. A.P. French and P.J. Kennedy, Cambridge: Harvard University Press.

O'Connor, T., 2002 (January 7), *Free Will*, retrieved 14 December 2017, from *Stanford Encyclopedia of Philosophy*: https://plato.stanford.edu/entries/freewill/.

Paulson, S., 2017 (May 4), *Roger Penrose on Why Consciousness Does Not Compute*, retrieved 18 June 2018, from Nautilus: https://nautil.us/issue/47/consciousness/roger-penrose-on why-consciousness-does-not-compute.

Pokharna, S.S., 1985, "A New Investigation into the Problem of Perfect Determinism in Modern Science", *Indian Philosophical Quarterly*, XII(1): 67-84.

——, 2008, "Science Technology and New Paradigm of Philosophy: Modern Interpretation of Jain Philosophy", *Tirthankar Vani*, 8: 53-58; 9: 59-62; 10: 59-61 & 11; and 12: 3-75.

——, 2013a, "Exploration of General Systems Theory and Jain Philosophy Could Provide New Ways of Looking at the Field of Bioethics", *Syntropy* 2: 243-79, retrieved 24 August 2018, from http://www.sintropia.it/journal/english/2013-eng-2-18.pdf.

——, 2013b, "Limitations of Scientific Knowledge and the Concept of

Knowledge through Consciousness in Jain Philosophy", *Journal of Gyan Sagar Science Foundation*, 1(1): 24-33.

——, 2015, "Quantum Field Theory, Consciousness and Jainism", *The International Journal for Transformation of Consciousness*, 1(1): 319-31.

Prabhacandra, 1941, *Prameyakamal Martand*, ed. M.K. Shastri, Bombay: Nirnay Sagar Press.

Rahula, W., 2006, "Preface", in *What the Buddha Taught*, Sri Lanka: Buddhist Cultural Centre.

Rashdall, H., 1907, *The Theory of Good and Evil*, vol. II, Oxford: Clarendon Press

Rice, Hugh, "Fatalism", *Stanford Encyclopedia of Philosophy*, 18 December 2002. Web. 24 August 2018.

Shah, U.D., 2002, *Karan Karya Rahasya*, ed. M.R. Shah, Mumbai: Veetragvani Prakashak.

Sikdar, J.C., 1964, *Studies in Bhagwati Sutra*, vol. I, Muzaffarpur: Research Institute of Prakrit, Jainology and Ahimsa.

Singh, R., 1974, *Jaina Concept of Omniscience*, Ahmedabad: L.D. Institute of Indology.

Sogani, K.C., 1993, *Samaṇasuttam*, Text and English translation, vol. I, Jaipur: Prakrit Bharati Academy.

——, 2001, *Ethical Doctrines in Jainism*, Solapur: Jain Sanskriti Sanrakshak Sangh.

——, 2008, *Spiritual Awakening (Sanyagdarśana) and other Essays*, Jaipur: Prakrit Bharati Academy.

——, 2013, "Religion and Morality (Ethics): Jaina Perspective", in *Study Notes (Selected Papers on Jainism)*, vol. II, pp. 195-202, New Delhi: International School for Jain Studies.

Surishwarji, A. (ed.), 2017, *Āvaśyaka Cūrṇi: Āvaśyaka Niryukti evaṁ Cūrṇi*, Paladi, Ahmedabad: Shri Param Anand Shwetambar Murtipujak Jain Sangh.

Sūtrakṛtāṅga-Jaina Sūtra, Part-II, tr. H. Jacoby, Delhi: Low Price Publications, 1996.

Suzuki, D., 2002, "Outlines of Mahayana Buddhism", in *Buddhanusmrti (A*

Glossary of Buddhist Terms), ed. A. Kala, pp. 120-21, Mumbai: Somaiya Publication.

Śvetāśvatara Upaniṣad, tr. M. Giri, Varanasi: Shri Dakshinamurti Math Prakashan, 1975.

Taylor, R., 2006, "Determinism: A Historical Survey", in *Encyclopedia of Philosophy*, ed. D.M Brochert, second edn, vol. III, pp. 4-23, New York: Thomson Gale.

Thomas, F. (ed.), 2014, *The Pravacanasāra of Kundakunda Ācārya: Together with the Commentary, Tattva-dīpikā, by Amr̥tacandra Sūri*, New York: Cambridge University Press.

Todarmal, 2005, *Mokshamarg Prakashak*, ed. J. Jain, Bombay: Shri Kund-Kund Kahan Digamber Jain Tirth Suraksha Trust.

Umāsvāti/Umasvami, 1994, *Tattvārthasūtra: That Which Is*, *tr.* N. Tatia, Delhi: Motilal Banarsidass.

——, 2000, *Tattvārthasūtra*, tr. K.K. Dixit, Ahmedabad: L.D. Institute of Indology.

——, 2011, *Tattvārthasūtra*, ed. V.K. Jain, Dehradun: Vikalp Printers.

Vallely, A., 2002, *Guardians of the Transcendent: An Ethnography of a Jain Ascetic Community*, Toronto: University of Toronto Press.

Van Gigch, J.P., 1978, *Applied General Systems Theory*, New York: Harper and Row Publishers.

Varni, J., 1993, *Samaṇa Suttam*, ed. S. Jain, and tr. T.K. Tukol and K.K. Dixit, Varanasi: Sarva Seva Sangh Prakashan.

Walpola, R., 1972, *What the Buddha Taught*, London: Gordon Fraser.

Williams, P., 2008, *Mahayana Buddhism: The Doctrinal Foundations*, New York: Routledge.

Wikipedia contributors, 2021 (13 April), *Determinism*, retrieved 15 April, 2021, from Wikipedia, The Free Encyclopedia: https://en.wikipedia.org/wiki/Determinism

शास्त्रवार्त्तासमुच्चय, आचार्य हरिभद्र, अनु० कृष्ण कुमार दीक्षित, लालभाई दलपतभाई भारतीय संस्कृति विद्यामन्दिर, अहमदाबाद, 2002।

जैन, श्वेता, 2008, *जैनदर्शन में कारण–कार्य व्यवस्था : एक समन्वयात्मक दृष्टिकोण*, पार्श्वनाथ विद्यापीठ, वाराणसी और प्राच्य विद्यापीठ, शाजापुर।

शास्त्री, बंशीधर, 1985, *भाग्य और पुरुषार्थ : एक नया अनुचिन्तन*, वीर सेवा मन्दिर ट्रस्ट, वाराणसी।

महाभारत (पंचम खण्ड), शान्तिपर्व, अनु० रामनारायणदत्त शास्त्री, गीताप्रेस, गोरखपुर, 2013।

सिंह, रामजी, 1993, *जैन दर्शन : चिन्तन–अनुचिन्तन*, जैन विश्व भारती, लाडनूं।

श्वेताश्वतरोपनिषद्, अनु० महेशानन्द गिरी, श्री दक्षिणामूर्ति मठ प्रकाशन, वाराणसी, 1975।

शास्त्रवार्त्तासमुच्चय और उसकी व्याख्या – स्याद्वादकल्पलता का हिन्दी विवेचन (स्तबक 2), अनु० बदरीनाथ शुक्ल, दिव्यदर्शन ट्रस्ट, मुम्बई, 1979।

शिशुपालवध महाकाव्यम्, अनु० रामप्रताप त्रिपाठी, भारतीय विद्या संस्थान, वाराणसी, 2010।

श्रीमद्वाल्मीकीय रामायण (भाग 1), अनु० जानकीनाथ शर्मा, गीताप्रेस, गोरखपुर, 2012।

भारिल्ल हुकुमचन्द, *क्रमबद्ध पर्याय*, पण्डित टोडरमल स्मारक ट्रस्ट, जयपुर, 2016।

सन्मतितर्क प्रकरण, सिद्धसेन दिवाकर, ज्ञानोदय ट्रस्ट, अहमदाबाद, 1969।

Contributors

Dr Surendra S. Pokharna worked as a senior scientist at Space Applications Centre, Ahmedabad (Indian Space Research Organization) for about nineteen years. Worked as Chief Operating Officer at Juriscape Pvt Ltd, under Hitech Outsourcing services company of Ahmedabad and currently acting as Consultant in same company. Also worked as Assistant Professor and Lecturer in Physics in three colleges for about eight years. Developed websites in Hindi and Rajasthani, viz. www.kranti1857.org and www.aapanorajashan.org. Interested in doing research in interdisciplinary fields like physics, operations research, system sciences, Indian culture, Jainism, etc. Has published about one hundred publications in physics, operations research, remote sensing, sustainable development, Indian culture, Jainism, etc.
E-mail: sspokharna15@yahoo.com

Dr Prakash C. Kanthaliya, former Professor and Head, Dept. of Agricultural Chemistry and Soil Science, Maharana Pratap University of Agriculture & Technology, Udaipur (Rajasthan). He has completed various research projects as the Principal Investigator. Kanthaliya was elected as Councillor of Indian Society of Soil Science for two years (2003-04). He was nominated as Member of National Monitoring Team by Goverment of India in 2004-05 to increase production of cotton.
E-mail: pckanthaliya@gmail.com

Dr Shugan C. Jain has pursued, since 2002, full-time Jain studies (earned PhD) and then, in 2005, promoted International School for Jain Studies (www.isjs.in) to introduce academic studies of Jainism

primarily in universities of North America. He has published several books and research papers on Jainism. Prior to the above tasks, Jain worked as Information and System Consultant/Director/ entrepreneur during 1962–2002 in India, USA and the Netherlands.
E-mail: shuganjain1941@gmail.com

Dr Christopher Key Chapple, Doshi Professor of Indic and Comparative Theology and Founding Director of the Master of Arts in Yoga Studies at Loyola Marymount University, Los Angeles, CA. He has more than twenty books to his credit. Chapple serves on the advisory boards of the South Asian Studies Association, the Forum on Religion and Ecology (Yale), the Ahimsa Center (Pomona), the Jain Studies Centre (SOAS, London), the Dharma Academy of North America (Berkeley) and the International School for Jain Studies, Pune.
E-mail: christopherkeychapple@gmail.com

Dr Bimalendra Kumar did his PhD in Buddhist Studies from the University of Delhi in 1990 and has been teaching since then for thirty years in various universities such as the University of Delhi, Vishva Bharati University, Santiniketan and Banaras Hindu University, Varanasi. Currently, he is working as a Professor and Head, Department of Pali & Buddhist Studies, Faculty of Arts, Banaras Hindu University. His areas of interest are Pali, Theravāda Buddhism, Buddhist Philosophy (Abhidhamma Philosophy) and Tibetan Buddhism. He has been on numerous academic bodies of universities and institutes and other academic bodies, and as a member of the governing boards of the organizations.
E-mail: bimalendrakumar9@gmail.com

Dr Meenal Katarnikar, Associate Professor of Philosophy, University of Mumbai. She did her PhD in Philosophy from Mumbai University in 1997 and Post-Doctoral on "The Jain Theory of Parokṣa Pramāṇa: A Critical Approach" in 2001 from the same university. Her areas of interest are Epistemology, Indian Philosophy especially, Jainism, Buddhism and Vedānta, Research Methodology

and Kauṭilya Arthaśāstra. She has three books and more than thirty-five research papers to her credit.
E-mail: mili21mili@yahoo.co.uk

Dr Kamini Gogri is a Philosophical Counsellor based in Mumbai. She is MA and PhD in Philosophy and History from the University of Mumbai. Gogri is a Project Fellow on Jain Prosopography at Centre of Jain Studies, School of Orient and African Studies, London. Her areas of expertise are Social History, Modern History, Cultural Studies, Epistemology, Ethics and Gender History. She has been the visiting faculty at Department of Philosophy, University of Mumbai, Mumbai.
E-mail: kaminigogri@gmail.com

Dr Navin Kumar Srivastav, Assistant Curator, Jain Museum Project, Amar Prerana Trust, Pune. He is MA and PhD in Philosophy from Banaras Hindu University. He was awarded General Fellowship from Indian Council of Philosophical Research (ICPR), New Delhi and Junior Fellowship from Ministry of Culture, Goverment of India. Srivastav has been Research Associate at Parshwanath Vidyapeeth, Varanasi and the Joint Director at International School for Jain Studies. He has been published more than fifteen research papers on various aspects of Jainology.
E-mail: navinsrivastav@shrifirodiatrust.org

Jinesh R. Sheth, an enthusiastic research scholar currently pursuing PhD on "A Critical Study of Anekāntavāda" from Department of Philosophy, the University of Mumbai. His specialization is in Epistemology, Applied Philosophy, Relativism, Jain Philosophy. His areas of interests include Indian Philosophy, Scepticism, Philosophy of Science, Ancient Greek Philosophy, Analytic Philosophy, Logic, Hermeneutics, Existentialism, Consciousness Studies, Ethics, Metaphilosophy and Philosophy as a Way of Life.
E-mail: jineshrsheth13@gmail.com

Dr Rahul Kumar Singh, Lecturer of Logic at Bajarang Inter College, Kunda, Pratapgarh (UP). He is MA and PhD in Philosophy from

Banaras Hindu University. He was awarded General Fellowship from Indian Council of Philosophical Research (ICPR), New Delhi. Singh has been Research Associate at Parshwanath Vidyapeeth, Varanasi and has been published more than twelve research papers on various aspects of Jainology.
E-mail: dr.rahulkrsingh@gmail.com

Index

abandonment of ego as the key to freedom 62

abhavya 35

absolute
- doctrine of 20
- fatalism 127
- God, existence of 111
- indeterminism 115
- *karma*-determinism 114
- non-absolutism 131

abuddhipūrvaka 128

Ācārya
- Bhikṣu 71
- Kundakunda 38, 45, 61-65, 119
- Malliṣenasūri 120
- Māṇikyanandi 120
- Nanesh 3, 11
- Prabhācandra 120
- Samantabhadra 114-15, 119, 127-28, 131
- Siddhasena vii, 121
- Tulsī 72

Ācārāṅgasūtra 45-47, 49-51, 86

ācāryas 72

act of will to undo the will 65

action
- 180 forms of 56
- centrality of 58
- rightness of 41

adharma 23, 35

adhyavasana 64

Ādinātha 27

Adṛṣṭavādī 112

Advaita Vedānta 57, 59

aesthetic practices of Jain *yoga* 60

agnosticism 18

agurulaghu 26

ahiṁsā 18, 41, 67, 86-88, 97
- comprehensive definitions of 86
- concept of 97
- doctrine of 88
- Jain
  - concept of 86
  - principle of 87

ajara-amara 26

ajīva 34-35, 125, 129

Ājīvika 17-18
- metaphysics 20
- movement 20
- philosophy 20
- school of thought 20

Ājīvakas vii, 110-11

ajñāna 17-19
philosophy 18
ākāśa 23, 35
akuppācetovimutti 79
all
scientific measurements, foundation of 6
virtues, virtue of 86
Amṛtacandra 125, 130
ananta ānanda 26
anantavīrya 26
anātman 19
anattā 19
anekānta 42
Anekāntavāda vii, 86, 89, 91, 116, 127, 130-31
is a central thought of Jainism 88
Aṅguttara Nikāya viii, 79-80
antarāya 24
karma 26
antinomian ethics 18
anubhāva 25
*aṇuvrata*s 40
Āptamīmāṁsā 114, 120, 127-28, 131
Aquinas, St. Thomas 115
*arhant*s 72
arhat 61
*arhat*s 86, 119-20
Aristotle 51
artha paryāya 34
arūpī 26
asat 59
asceticism is the ideal path of life 84
asiddha 40
āsrava 35
Aṣṭasahasrī 120
Aṣṭaśatī 120
āstika 17
aśubha-karma 62
atheism 18
atheists 20
Ātmakhyāti 130
ātman 19-20
atomic energy 1
atomism 18
attitude of resignation 31
audārika 36
auspicious
body 56
lifespan 56
status 56
austerity 56
authority of the Vedas 20
Āvaśyaka Cūrṇi 22
Āvaśyakasūtra 110
Ayer, A.J. 127
ayoga 59
āyu karma 40
āyuṣya karma 26

Babb, Lawrence 72
baddha 25, 38
Bālā 60
bala 79
bandha 23, 35
Barua, B.M. 20
Basham, A.L. 20-22

basic assumption of Jainism 89
beneficial *karma*, inflow of 53
Bhagavadgītā 66
Bhagavatīsutra 110
bhāgya 37
bhakti 70
Bhandari, N. 3
Bharil, Hukam Chand viii, 38
Bhattacharya, R. 18
bhāva 21, 39, 64
  karmas 39
bhāvas 64
Bhave, Vinoba 65
bhavya 35
biological systems 2, 6-7
biotechnology 1
births and
  deaths, cycles of 66
  rebirths, cycle of 22
Blackburn, S. 38
bliss 46
bodhisattva 90
Bohm, D. 13
bojjhaṅga 79
bondage 41, 51, 97
  and liberation, Jain theory of 97
  of *karmas* to the soul 24
Bowker, J. 17
Brahmā 45
Brahman, Vedic concept of 19
brahmavihāra 76
Bryant, Edwin F. 73
Buchanan, M. 9
Buddha 57, 75-77, 80-81, 91
Buddhacarita viii
Buddhavacana 80
buddhipūrvaka 128
Buddhism viii, 18-19, 45, 57, 59, 75, 77, 79-81, 83, 85, 109, 111
  teachings of 58
Buddhist 17
  doctrines 58
  ethics 76
  philosophy 19
  theory of dependent origination 76
  thought 90
  tradition 86, 90
Buddhists 59
byāpāda 80

caitanya 62
Cārvāka 17-18
  philosophy 18
Cārvākas 20
Cārvākins 47
causal theory 112
causality 2
  law of 13
causation
  theories of 112
  theory of 109
cause 32
  and effect, universal law of 23
cause–effect relationship 40
central concept of Hinduism and Jainism 20
centrality of action 58
cetanā is equated with *kamma* 82

Chakravarty, A. 125
chanda 78
Chapple, C.K. 58
characteristic of
  dravya 34
  non-violence 87
Chrysippus 121
classic physics 7
classical physics 2, 6
Close, E.R. 4, 13
closed
  isolated system 6
  systems 2, 6
co-destined facts, theory of 121
coexistence of free will and determinism 126
commercialization 1
comparative approaches to spiritual discipline 57
compartmentalization 2
compassion 91, 94
  spirit of 90
compatibilism 127, 131
complete knowledge of metaphysics 19
comprehensive definitions of *ahiṁsā* 86
concept of
  ahiṁsā 97
  determinism 3-4, 9, 11
  freedom 75, 115
  indeterminism 8
  knowledge 3
    of Indian philosophy 3
  soul 18
conception of determinism 113
conduct-deluding *karma* 54
consciousness 46
  dimensions of 13
  higher stages of 10
  manifestation of 63
  states of 62
conservation laws
  definitions of 6
  of physics 6
continence 56
control 47
conventional decision theory 8
core ethical issues 83
cosmic
  power destiny 113
  ruling principle of 109
creation, cycles of 110
creative powers of each individual 57
Cullavagga 80-81
cycle of
  births and
    deaths 66
    rebirths 22
  creation 110
  life and death and rebirth 61

darśanāvaraṇīya 24
Dasti, Matthew R. 73
decision-making process 4
definitions of conservation laws 6
departed saints, lives of 73
Descartes, René 37
detachment 56, 91
deterioration of political standards 93

determinism vii, 2, 7, 10, 14, 31, 84, 114, 116, 119-21, 123, 125-26, 128-31
  and free will, problem of 84
  concept of 3-4, 9, 11
  conception of 113
  general characteristics of 84
  variance of 11
determinist theories 129
deterministic theories 76
devaluation of social morality 93
devotionalism 71
Dhamma 80
Dhammapada 81
dharma 17, 19, 23, 35
Digambara(s) 45, 50, 61
Dīgha Nikāya viii, 77, 80
Dīgha Nikāya–Samaññaphala Sutta 110
dimensions of
  consciousness 13
  dimensions of
    space 13
    time 13
Diodorus 121
Diprā 60
direct evidence of materialistic life 18
discipline 91
dissociation 41
Divākara, Siddhasena 37, 111
diverse range of heterodox beliefs 17
divine will 60
Dixit, K.K. 116, 124
doctrine of
  absolute determinism 20
  ahiṁsā 88
  fatalism 109
  fatalists 32
  free will 75-76, 110
  karma vii, 84, 113
  non-violence 88
Doniger, W. 17
Doshi, R.L. 22
Draupadī 72
dravya 34
  characteristic of 34
Dravyasaṁgraha 34, 36
dveṣa 62, 64

each individual, creative powers of 57
early Buddhism 18, 20
economic development 1
effect 32
  of the *karma*s 115
efficacy of human
  action 59
  effort 65
effort 78
ego as the key to freedom, abandonment of 62
ehipassika 80
eight
  forms of *karma* 51
  kinds of *karma*s 65
  types of reality-shaping *karma*s 52
eightfold path 77, 90
Einstein 12
electronics 1

emphasis on spiritual values 93
empirical soul, future state of 39
empiricism 2
energy 46, 78
environmental determinism 84
equanimity 67, 69
essential prerequisites of interpersonal relations 95
eternal soul, rejection of 19
ethical
- guidance 94
- theories, foundational ground for 86
- theory 20

ethical behaviour 69
- of the highest order 67

everything, theory of 13
existence of absolute God 111
external possessions, renunciation of 69
extreme
- asceticism, idealization of 18
- rigours of Jain monastic life 70

fast unto death 56
fatalism vii, 18, 21, 31-33, 111, 127
- doctrine of 109
- theory of 18

fatalists 32
- doctrine of 32

final release, goal of 69
five
- *bhāvas* 124
- causes 124
- equals 28
- essentials 26, 28
- exemplary communities 72
- great vows 65
- indulgences 53
- major vows 56
- senses 53
- theories of causation 111

fivefold
- causal theory 121
- controlling factors 79

forbidden behaviour 58
forest gods 52
foundation of all scientific measurements 6
foundational ground for the ethical theories 86
four
- characteristics of *karmas* 24
- passions 53
- varieties of white meditation 57

fourfold efforts 77
free arising of wisdom 80
free will 14, 18, 109, 119-20, 126, 128
- and determinism, coexistence of 126
- philosophy of 50

freedom 64
- are sixteenfold 55
- concept of 75, 115
- notion of 126

freedom of
- choice 76, 78
- expression 81

freedom through wisdom 80
future state of an empirical soul 39

intrinsic element of 6

Indian
- doctrine of *karma* 109
- fatalism 20
- philosophy 11, 13
- poet-saints 71

individual soul 87

indriyāṇi 77

indriyas 79

induction 2

infinite
- bliss 23
- intuition 23
- knowledge 23
- power 23

inflow of beneficial *karma* 53

influx 41
- of new *karma* 24

inner purity 63

instrumental cause is extrinsic in nature 122

inter-denominational dialogue within the Jain communities 65

internal resolve on non-attachment 69

inter-personal relations, essential prerequisites of 95

intrinsic
- and extrinsic nature of *jīva* 38
- decision-making process 8
- element of indeterminism 6

intuition-covering *karmas* 54

issaranimmānahetu viii

Īśvara 57

īśvara-tantra 112

Jain 17
- communities, inter-denominational dialogue within 65
- concept of *ahiṁsā* 86
- doctrine 42
  - of *karma* 111
- ethics 41
- *karma* theory 4
- monastic life, extreme rigours of 70
- notion of omniscience 120
- path of purification 52
- philosophy 3, 23
  - and religion, unique character of 88
- principle of *ahiṁsā* 87
- purification 46
- soteriology 97
- theory of bondage and liberation 97
- tradition 86
- vows 73
- will, ultimate act of 56
- *yoga*, aesthetic practices of 60

Jaini, P.S. 25

Jainism viii, 18-20
- Anekāntavāda is a central thought of 88
- basic assumption of 89
- historical and mythical literature of 41
- normative aspects of 41

Jains, religious observances of 70

Jambū/Jambūdvīpa 52 61

Jayatilleke, K.N. 18, 76

jina 67, 72
- victors 46

jīva 23, 28, 35, 37, 39-40, 45, 60, 125, 129-30
intrinsic and extrinsic nature of 38
jīvas 36, 42, 46
jñāna 124
jñānāvaraṇa 124
jñānāvaraṇīya 24
Johnson, W.J. 62, 64-65

Kabīr 71
Kachhara, N.L. 9
kāla viii, 23, 35, 37, 111-12
kālalabdhi 27
kālāma 79-80
Kālāmasutta 79
Kālavādī 111
kāla-viśeṣa 111
Kalpasūtra 50
kāmacchanda 80
kamma viii, 81
cetanā is equated with 82
kammic determinism viii
kaṇayamaṇaṇṇamiha 125
Kāntā 60
karma 17, 19-20, 39, 45, 50-52, 54, 60, 66-67, 69, 110, 114, 120, 122-23
eight forms of 51
Indian doctrine of 109
Jain doctrine of 111
particles 87
purging of 55
reality of 58
realm of 65
soul of 73
stream of 46
theory 9, 28, 57, 123, 130
karma theory of
Jain philosophy 9
Jainism 23, 26
karma-bandha 23
karma-determinism 85, 114
karman bondage 24
kārmaṇa vargaṇā 23
karmas 11, 35, 46, 112, 115-16, 124
effect of 115
eight kinds of 65
four characteristics of 24
have four characteristics 9
to the soul, bondage of 24
upayoga of 64
kārmic 36, 51
activities 37
causality 45
fruition 124
influence 115
obstructions 61
particles 23
karuṇā 76, 86, 90
kaṣāya 23
kāyika yoga 88
kāyotsarga 68
Kelting, W. 70-72
kevala 46
darśana 25
jñāna 25
jñānī 13
Knapton, S. 1
knowledge
concept of 3
of Indian philosophy, concept of 3

Kothari, D. 7
krama 34
kramabaddha paryāya 38
kriyā 47
Kṛṣṇa 72
kṣaya 39
kṣayopaśamika 39
kṣetra 38
kusalassaupasampadā 81

law of causality 13
liberation 50, 67, 97
  path of 59
life
  and death and rebirth, cycle of 61
  asceticism is the ideal path of 84
limitations of scientific methodology 3
linear momentum 6
lives of the departed saints 73
Lokāyata 18
Lord Mahāvīra 21-22, 27, 32, 46, 49-51, 57, 61, 88, 110
  tradition of 58
Lord Pārśvanātha 46, 71
luminous gods 52

madhyamā pratipada 86, 91
mahā-karuṇā citta 91
Mahāparinibbāna Sutta 80
Mahataṇhāsaṅkhayasutta 78
mahāvratas 41
Mahāyāna Buddhism 90
Majjhima Nikāya 78-80
Malalasekera, G. 77
male monasticism 49
man's final goal 85
mānasika 88
Mandāra mountain 66
manifestation of consciousness 63
mantras 72
manufacturing 1
materialism 18
materialistic life, direct evidence of 18
mathematical formalism 8
means of purification 47
mechanism 2
meditation 17, 20, 65, 69
Mehta, M.L. 23, 25
metaphysical
  determinism 123, 130
  soul 18
  theories 89
metaphysics, complete knowledge of 19
mettā 76
middha 80
middle path 94
Mīmāṁsā 17
Mirābāī 71
mithyā 37
Mitrā 60
modern agriculture 1
moha 62, 64, 81
mohanīya karma 26

mokṣa 11, 19, 27, 32, 35, 84-85, 87, 124
mokṣa-oriented Śramaṇa ethics 95
Monier-Williams, M. 46
moral
  action 81
  bankruptcy 93
  freedom 81
  values 94
moral responsibility 120, 128
  problem of 119
mukhya pratyakṣa 120
multiple dimensions of time 4
mysterious cosmic power 109

Nagel, Thomas 37-38
Nahar, P.C. 116
nāma 24
  karma 26
ṇamokāra mantra 72
nāstika 17
nature of pure soul 40
Nayavāda 88
Neppe, V.M. 4, 13
new *karma*, influx of 24
Newton's law(s) of motion 7, 11
nibbāna 79, 90-91
*nidhatta karma*s 25
niggantha 32
nikācita 40
  *karma*s 25
nimitta 27-28, 37-38
nimittakāraṇa 114
nine
  quasi passions 54
  types of penance 57
nine-dimensional model of reality 13
nirjarā 35, 59
nirvāṇa 19-20
niścaya 62
niyati vii-viii, 20-21, 27-28, 37, 111-12, 122
Niyativāda vii-viii, 19-21, 26, 31, 39-40, 42, 109-11, 113, 119-20
  theory of 22
Niyativādī 112
non-deterministic causal conditioning, theory of 76
non-martial metaphors 66
non-possessiveness 91, 93
non-violence 47, 91, 93-94
  characteristic of 87
normative aspects of Jainism 41
notion of
  freedom 126
  origination–destruction and permanence 36
  self 65
nuclear wars 1
Nyāya 17

O'Connor, T. 126
omniscience 119
  Jain notion of 120
open systems 2, 6
orthodox philosophy, schools of 17
overmastering fate 109

padārthas 36
pañca-samavāya vii, 121
pañca-skandha 76
pañcindriya-bhāvanā 79
paññā 79
paññāvimutti 80
paññindriya 78-79
pāpa 67
 karma 64
parā 60, 64
Paramātman 61-62
Paramātmāprakāśa 60
parapsychology 10
parasamaya 39
Parīkṣāmukham 120
pariṇāma 21
pāriṇāmika 39
 bhāva 124
paryāya 34, 36, 38, 120, 122-24
paryāyas 37
passivism 2
path of liberation 59
paths for spiritual salvation 83
paṭiccasamuppanna 76-77
Paulson, S. 8
penance 47
 nine types of 57
Penrose, Roger 4, 8
perfect determinism 4-5
 possibility of 12
perfect forgiveness 56
permissibility of violence and meat-eating 18
perpetual consciousness 46
perseverance 78
personal improvement 65
philosophical propositions, truth value of 18
philosophy of
 free will 50
 voluntarism and free will 55
photoelectric effect 7
physical systems 7
physics, conservation laws of 6
Planck's constant 7
political standards, deterioration of 93
possibility of perfect determinism 12
potential spiritual status of women 50
power of will 65
Prabhā 60
practices of right view 63
pradeśa 24
Prajāpati 45
prakṛti 24, 26, 46
pramāda 87
Prameyakamalamārtaṇḍa 120
prārabdha vii
pratikramaṇa 41, 68
pratyākhyāna 68
Pravacanasāra 45, 61, 63, 119, 125
pre-destination 109
pre-determinism vii, 20, 31
premeditation 128
principle of supernatural power 18
probability function 8

problem of
  determinism and free will 84
  moral responsibility 119
process of wilful activity 59
psychological strengths, weakening of 93
psychology 10, 14
pubbekatahetu viii
pudgala 23, 35-36, 39
puṇya 67
  karma 65
Pūrana Kassapa 19
pure consciousness 79
pure soul 26, 32, 35
  nature of 40
  true powers of 9
purging of *karma* 55
purification
  Jain path of 52
  means of 47
purificatory process 58
purity 56, 64
  of the soul 56
puruṣa viii, 113
puruṣārtha vii, 27-28, 37, 111, 114
Puruṣārthavādī 112
pūrvakṛta viii
  adṛṣṭa 111

quantum
  mechanics 8, 12-13
  physics 3, 7, 11
  system 8

radical Indian scepticism 18
rāga 62, 64, 81
Rashdall, H. 115
Ratnakaraṇḍa Śrāvakācāra 131
reality of
  human freedom 76
  karma 58
  soul and matter 58
reality, nine-dimensional model of 13
reality-shaping *karmas*, eight types of 52
realization 65
realm of *karma* 65
reductionism 2
reincarnation 17
  of souls 110
rejection of an eternal soul 19
relativism 130
religious
  observances of Jains 70
  willpower 71
renunciation 17, 49, 56
  of external possessions 69
resignation, attitude of 31
Rice, Hugh 32
right
  action 63
  conduct 67
    theory of 97
  knowledge 63
  thought 63
rightness of the action 41
ṛtu-bheda 111
ruling principle of the cosmic process 109

sabbapāpassa akaraṇaṁ 81

saddhābala 79
saddhindriya 78-79
sādhu(s) 63-64, 72
*sādhvī*s 72
sakāyaniruttiyā 81
salvation 111
  of the soul 24
samādhi 58, 79
samādhindriya 78-79
Samaṇa Suttam 45, 65-67, 69
*samavāya*s 27
samaya 42
Samayasāra 45, 61, 63-64, 125
Samayasāra-Kalaśa 130
sāmāyika 63, 68-69
Sāṁkhya 17, 66
  system 62
Sāṁkhyā-kārikā 57
sammāvāyāma 77
saṁsāra 19, 35, 63, 65
saṁsārī jīva 36
saṁvara 35
*samvāya*s 37
samyak saṅkalpa 90
saṅgati 21
Saṅgha 80-81
saṅkhārakkhandha 76
Sanmatitarka 111
Sanmatitarka Prakaraṇa vii, 37, 121
santhārā 70
sarvajña 38
sat 34, 59
satindriya 78-79
Schlick, Moritz 127
schools of
  heterodox philosophy 17
  orthodox philosophy 17
Schrodinger's equation 8
science on the society and the environment, total deterministic effect of 5
science-related developments 2
scientific methodology 5
  limitations of 3
scientific understanding of a phenomenon 6
self
  is the doer of all actions 66
  notion of 65
self-built kārmic world 66
self-determinism 115
self-effort 32, 45, 116
self-realization 95
self-reflecting 84
self-reliance 32
self-restraint 47, 55-56
seven supplementary observances 56
Shah, U.D. 38
siddha 35, 61
siddhaloka 52
Siddhārtha Gautama 19
*siddha*s 72, 124
Siddhasena 116
Sikdar, J.C. 113
*śikṣāvrata*s 41
Singh, R. 120

six
 external austerities 57
 internal austerities 57
 obligatory duties 68
skandha 62
social
 morality, devaluation of 93
 systems 2, 6-7, 12
 uplift 65
Sogani, K.C. 41, 61
soul 52
 concept of 18
 of *karma* 73
 purity of 56
 salvation of 24
 true nature of 65
soul has
 a material form 20
 consciousness 52
soul is
 formless 19-20
 omnipresent 19
souls, reincarnation of 110
space
 dimensions of 13
 technology 1
space–time invariance condition 4
spanda 52
spatial displacement 6
spirit of compassion 90
spiritual
 discipline, comparative approaches to 57
 goals 45
 perfection 76
 purifications 59
 values, emphasis on 93
spiritual salvation 91
 paths for 83
spṛṣṭa or *śithila karma*s 25
śramaṇa 85
Śramaṇa ethics 83, 91, 93, 95
Śramaṇas 32-33
states of consciousness 62
stavana 71
Sthirā 60
sthiti 24
stoppage 41
straightforwardness 56
stream of *karma* 46
strong will 78
Stuti-Vidyā 131
śubha 41
śuddha 62
śuddhopāyayoga 63
suffering 17
sukha 62
śūnyatā 91
supernatural power, principle of 18
supreme
 dharma 86
 victory 66
Sūrdās 71
Sūtrakṛtāṅga 32-33, 115
svabhāva viii, 21, 37, 111-12
Svabhāvavādī 112
Svayambhū-Stotra 131
Śvetāmbara(s) 45, 50
Śvetāśvatara Upaniṣad 112-13
Syādvāda vii, 88, 116

Syādvāda Mañjarī 120

Tantra 57
tapas 50
Tārā 60
Tattvārthasūtra 23-24, 34-35, 39, 45, 50-51, 54-56, 86-87, 122-24, 129
*tattva*s 35, 41, 97
Taylor 121, 123, 126
teachings of Buddhism 58
tejas 36
telecommunication 1
ten mansion gods 52
Terāpantha
  order 71
  Śvetāmabara community 70, 72
terrorism 1
theistic determinism viii
theme of freedom 64
theological determinism 84, 122, 130
theories of causation 112
theory of
  causation 109
  co-destined facts 121
  everything 13
  fatalism 18
  Niyativāda 22
  non-deterministic causal conditioning 76
  right conduct 97
thīnamiddha 80
thinking in relation to action 81
Thomas, F. 126
time
  dimensions of 13
  multiple dimensions of 4
tīrthaṅkara 27, 41
tīrthaṅkaranāma karma 40
*tīrthaṅkara*s 46, 72
Todarmal 124
total
  deterministic effect of science on the society and the environment 5
  freedom 60
  nudity 49
tradition of Lord Mahāvīra 58
transcendent spiritual goal 95
tri-ratna 97
true
  nature of the soul 65
  powers of a pure soul 9
truth 93
  value of philosophical propositions 18
truthfulness 56
twenty-five urges 53
twenty-four
  *jina*s 68
  *tīrthaṅkara*s 70
twenty-two hardships 56
types of knowledge 11

udaya 39
ultimate
  act of Jain will 56
  goal of liberation 17
Umāsvāti 45, 50-51, 58, 86
unique character of the Jain philosophy and religion 88

universal
  law of cause and effect 23
  laws supporting Niyativāda 41
upādāna 37
upādhyāyas 72
Upadhye 60
Upāsaka-daśāṅgasūtra 113
upaśama 39
upayoga 35
  of *karmas* 64
ussāha 78
Uvāsagadasāo 113

vācika 88
vaikriyaka 36
Vaiśeṣika 17
Vajjians 80
Vallely, Anne 70
value crisis 93
vandanā 68
vargaṇās 39
variance of determinism 11
vastu 33
vāyāma 78
vedanīya 24
vedanīya karma 26
Vedānta 17, 59
Vedāntins 59
Vedas 17
  authority of 20
Vedic
  concept of *Brahman* 19
  tradition 109
vegetarianism 18
Vibhajjavāda 91
vicikicchā 80
view-deluding *karma* 54
vimāṁsā 78
Viṁśati-viṁśikā Prakaraṇam 112
violence and meat-eating, permissibility of 18
viriya 78
viriyabala 79
viriyindriya 78-79
virtue of all virtues 86
vīrya 62
Visuddhimagga 57
vītarāga 26
voluntarism and free will, philosophy of 55
vratas 42
vrātyas 32
Vyākhyāprajñapti 22
vyañjana paryāya 34
vyavahāra 62, 64

Walpola, R. 75, 92
weakening of the psychological strengths 93
white meditation, four varieties of 57
wilful
  activity, process of 59
  karma 55
will 45, 78
  is *cetanā* 81
  power of 65
Williams, P. 19

wisdom
  free arising of 80
  potential spiritual status of 50

yadṛcchā 112

yoga 17, 59-60
Yoga tradition 45
Yogadṛṣṭisamuccaya 45, 57-58, 60
Yogasūtra 57
Yogindu 60